A Small City in France

Françoise Gaspard

◆ ◆ ◆

Translated by
Arthur Goldhammer

Harvard University Press
Cambridge, Massachusetts
and London, England
1995

Copyright © 1995 by the President and Fellows of Harvard College
All rights reserved
Printed in the United States of America
Original French edition: *Une Petite Ville en France,*
copyright © Editions Gallimard, 1990

Publication of this book has been aided by a grant from
The French Ministry of Culture.

This book is printed on acid-free paper, and its binding materials
have been chosen for strength and durability.

Library of Congress Cataloging-in-Publication Data
Gaspard, Françoise.
[Petite ville en France. French]
A small city in France / Françoise Gaspard; translated by Arthur Goldhammer.
p.   cm.
Includes bibliographical references and index.
ISBN 0-674-81096-1 (cloth)
ISBN 0-674-81097-X (pbk.)
1. Dreux (France)—Politics and government. 2. Front national
(France, 1972–)—Influence. 3. Elections—France—Dreux.
4. France. Parlement (1946–). Assemblée nationale—Elections,
1989. I. Title.
DC801.D79G37 1995
944′.51—dc20

94-12460
CIP

A Small City in France

Contents

Foreword by Eugen Weber

In July 1821, a nineteen-year-old poet set out on foot from Paris to woo the girl he loved and who loved him. Her parents, who opposed the marriage of young people with no expectations, had decided that renting a summer place in the environs of the capital, as they usually did, would bring the suitor running to spoil their holiday. They rented a house in Dreux instead, then a picturesque old township some sixty miles west of Paris on the road to Normandy (today's National Highway 12). A stagecoach ride that far cost twenty-five francs and Victor Hugo did not, they were sure, have twenty-five francs. But he had good legs. The Fouchers and their daughter, Adèle, left Paris on July 15; Hugo followed on the 16th. On the 19th he was in Dreux and on the 20th gained the parents' consent to his courtship. In 1822 Adèle Foucher became his wife; and a plaque on number 16 of the rue Godeau in Dreux commemorates his triumph, though the date it gives for the whirlwind visit is off by ten days. Why insist on accuracy in a romantic tale?

An inn still serves fine meals in the vale of Chérisy, three miles from the town center, where Hugo bathed in a stream beneath the birch trees and wrote a plangent poem about the sorrows of a lonely life. But Chérisy is no longer lonely. Dreux has grown out toward it, as it has grown all around.

It would take the townlet another eightscore years to reenter the history of France. But when it did, it did so with a bang. In 1983, municipal elections held there reverberated through the land when Jean-François Le Pen's National Front candidates won 16.7 percent of the votes cast, compared to 2.56 percent in 1981; and when, in coalition with more moderate right-wing groups, they took over the municipal council. Jean-Pierre Stirbois, one of the leaders of the Front, became assistant mayor. Dreux became more than a simple symbol of radical-right advances: it was a springboard for the Front's national success.

Municipal elections generally turn on local issues. In 1983, in the wake of the Socialist victory of 1981 and of the subsequent economic debacle, local and national issues happened to coincide. The Front's performance at Dreux could be a portent of things to come, and so it was to prove in the short run. In the European parliamentary elections of 1984, the National Front improved its Drouais showing further, to capture 19 percent of the vote. In 1989, a National Front woman candidate would be elected to the National Assembly from the Dreux region with over 61 percent of ballots cast. How could an erstwhile citadel of the moderate left and, briefly, of socialism have made so radical a turnabout?

Until the later 1950s, the town set in a bend of the Blaise River near the Eure had lived as it had always lived, closer to the rhythms of Victor Hugo's day than to those of Mitterrand and Le Pen. Its mayor from 1908 until his retirement in 1959 was Maurice Viollette, one of the great respectable figures of centrist socialism, best known for his ill-fated attempt in 1936 to grant citizenship and voting rights to Muslim Algerians. After Viollette's departure when he was eighty-eight, a right-wing coalition bent on urban growth and modern management began to develop the town: new industries, public housing projects, and real estate developments increased the population to over 30,000, but exacerbated local problems too.

Lying close to the Paris basin as it does (2,000 of its people travel to work in Paris every day), Dreux in the 1960s and 1970s experienced all the growing pains of a middling-small city expanding fast—too fast. From Hugo's day to 1950, the population had not even doubled; it doubled then in just twenty years and added another 10,000 in the 1970s. Growth outran urban equipment and traditional approaches to town management. The urban infrastructure sagged beneath demands for which it was not prepared. But right-wing gogetters, eager to attract taxpaying enterprises and to increase employment, were riding for a fall. In 1977, overwhelmed by intractable pressures on housing, traffic, schools, and social services, the right was turfed out. The left, led by a feisty local woman, Françoise Gaspard, conquered (or perhaps recaptured) the town hall, just in time to be hit full blast by the problems of the late seventies: soaring unemployment, careering immigration, and all the sociopolitical tensions wrought by their conjunction, notably an inclination to blame the town's troubles on its newcomers.

As early as 1971, *Le Monde* quoted the mayor of that day as expressing fears that the foreign population had reached the danger level, the *côte d'alerte*. Between 1975 and 1982, the French-born population of Dreux went down as the foreign-born population kept rising. The proportion of foreign residents— Turks, Portuguese, many North Africans—15 percent in 1975, stood at 21 percent in 1982, with concentrations as high as 60 percent in some parts of town. The proportion of foreign children in local schools varied from 6 percent in the center to as high as 72 percent in outlying housing projects, where half of the pupils were North Africans. A doctoral dissertation completed in 1983 spoke of the situation as "abnormal, extreme, excessive," and noted the creeping racism that it bred. Linking joblessness, delinquency, insecurity, and general social costs with invasive immigrants, Stirbois and his supporters cashed in on this: "What is the use of building at great expense schools, nurseries and cheap housing, when these are reserved not for the French who pay for them, but for the foreigners flowing in from every corner of the world? . . . How long will you accept being thrown out of your homes, out of your neighborhoods? . . . Don't be embarrassed to speak up: it's you who belong here!''

The backlash on which Stirbois and his allies rode to success was focused on Gaspard who, in the midst of economic crisis, had tried to reconcile French and non-French, natives and newcomers, and failed. More forthright and more determinedly socialist than Maurice Viollette, Gaspard was nevertheless his heir in terms of her social concerns and in certain aspects of her personality. "He had a difficult character," President Mitterrand said of Viollette, "which means that he had a lot of character." Gaspard had a lot of character too. Young, female, radical, a veteran of the restive sixties, she had also been elected to parliament as a Socialist deputy in 1981. Now she was denounced as a Marxist, a virago, and, of course, as an intellectual incapable of solving her town's problems, and only creating more. In the end, wearied and disgusted by a cruel, violent campaign, she stepped down as mayor even before the right-wing victories.

A historian by training, Gaspard today is back at her scholar's desk, writing and teaching at the Ecole d'Hautes Etudes en Sciences Sociales in Paris. *A Small City in France* is that rare commodity: a piece of history and social anthropology written by one of the principal actors in the events it recounts. The former mayor and deputy places her experience in historical context, both *courte* and *longue durée,* outlining the local past, the context and conditions of the conflict, and not least the traditional local orientation to center-left that made the National Front's breakthrough all the more striking. Gaspard describes society, economy, demography, and lets them explain what happened: slow growth between the wars, explosive growth after the 1950s, stagnation after the 1970s, the influx of foreign labor at first ignored amidst general upward mobility, then increasingly resented and, finally, as economic doldrums turned to serious crisis, condemned.

The greatest immigrant nation in the world after the United States, France has always relied on assimilation and integration. These no longer work. Faced with unassimilable numbers in a declining industrial economy, the great French tradition of cultural integration first cracked in the 1980s and then broke down. The people of Dreux had grudgingly tolerated French outsiders, then European ones. The inflow of Africans, especially North Africans, with their more marked "outsiderness," made their forerunners appear less unacceptable while focusing resentment almost exclusively on the latest, and most different, arrivals. Temporary industrial need, social indifference, even good intentions, were all outrun by escalating socioeconomic problems.

Françoise Gaspard's book is a document of our times, but also a parable *for* our times, even though the National Front tide is ebbing; regarded nationwide, it tends to crest at 11 or 12 percent of the vote. In Dreux as elsewhere in France, this radical-right vote appears as a protest against situations where urgent problems are not being solved—but also as an expression of feeling against the many people in positions of power who tend to dismiss frustrations and resentments as beside the point. This is the larger picture that the shaft of light cast by this book on one part of it can make a bit more comprehensible, as it comes to view in different contexts and in other nations.

Essential for students of twentieth-century France, this tale of a small town far away seems just as relevant to Americans caught up in their own problems and debates over surging immigration, racism, "America-first," and the like. Gaspard does not moralize, does not preach. Detached, scholarly, informative, and readable, her book provides material for reflection and, perhaps, regret.

Acknowledgments

Thanks to Birgitta Hessel, whose suggestion that I reread
William Sheridan Allen's *The Nazi Seizure of Power* led to my
writing this book; to l'Abbé Villette of Chartres and Madame
Edouard of Dreux, who kindly read over the sections on
Dreux's history; and to the newspaper *La République du centre*,
which made its files available to me.   F. G.

Translator's Note

Because of the complexities of French politics, I have silently
added brief explanations and designations to benefit the
non-French reader.   A. G.

"Six sympathizers of the extreme right, armed with blackjacks, baseball bats, a smoke grenade, knives, and a canister of tear gas, roamed through the center of town Monday night shouting 'Vive Le Pen!' 'Arabs out!' and 'France for the French!' and attacked nine youths (all French) from the Saint-Jean workers' dormitory on rue Godeau in Dreux. The assault left two people injured, one of them a young woman battered with 'Doc Martens,' the boot prized by so-called skinheads for its metal edges . . . The police arrested the six hoodlums on rue Godeau about twenty minutes after the assault, at 9:50 p.m. After all-night questioning, the individuals in custody confessed their involvement and identified themselves as sympathizers of the National Front."

—*L'Echo républicain*, 6 December 1989

The day before this incident, Marie-France Stirbois, the National Front candidate, was elected to the National Assembly from the second district of Eure-et-Loir, with an incredible 61.3 percent of the vote.

Revisiting Dreux

Dreux is a small city tucked away in the heart of France. For someone driving to Brest from Paris, which is less than an hour away, the town marks the almost imperceptible passage from the Ile-de-France region into Normandy. A motorist headed from Rouen toward the Loire enters the Beauce region right after leaving Dreux. But you have to pay attention: the landscape changes gently, and Dreux is hard to spot. Located at the junction of three river valleys, those of the Avre, the Eure, and the Blaise (the latter a stream that passes through the town itself), Dreux is a modest town, a subprefecture of the Eure-et-Loir département. Signs on the highway alert passing motorists that they are entering Dreux and a few miles later that they are leaving, and it's easy enough to exit the place without noticing that you've been there. The only signs of Dreux's existence are the rather ordinary buildings on its outskirts, just like those found on the outskirts of nearby cities such as Evreux and Chartres.

A small city? Some may question the adjective. By French standards Dreux ranks as a "medium-sized city," for it boasts slightly more than 30,000 inhabitants, this being the official criterion by which a town in France is no longer classified as small. The threshold was crossed around 1970, when times were good. But in 1982 the city had a hard time proving that it had not fallen back into the lesser category. This was a matter of some importance, for the size of subsidies from the national government depends on it, not to mention the salaries of municipal officials.

The same problems continued to plague city officials in 1990. During the most recent census, one of them, interviewed by a local paper, issued an appeal to the town's population that might seem surprising in light of the tense political climate at the time. All residents, including undocumented, clandestine aliens, were urged to demonstrate their civic spirit by cooperating with census takers: "Clandestine workers have every reason to do so, for they will be helping the city of Dreux. The greater the population, the more substantial the aid we will receive."[1] Three cheers for foreigners as long as their numbers help to fill city coffers! Preliminary estimates from the 1990 census put the population of Dreux at around 35,000. It is a small city nonetheless. Thirty or forty years ago its population stood between 12,000 and 15,000. The remnants of what used to be no more than a large town have not altogether disappeared. The old town lives on in local memory as a state of mind, a network of rumor, and a focal point of nostalgia. And those who remember the old town today share certain feelings of anxiety, fear, and anger.

All but unknown before 1980, Dreux became famous overnight. Television crews from many nations converged on the city. Jane Kramer contributed a long article on Dreux to *The New Yorker* (February 1986). The city's name came up in conversations between world leaders.[2] Nowadays, when travelers pass through Dreux, certain events, names, and images from that era will come to mind.

Dreux owes its recent celebrity not to its cheese or to its historical monuments or to some remarkable discovery made by one of its citizens. Its reputation comes from the substantial number of votes that the extreme right has been able to garner there over the past dozen years. With each new election, this number increases.

Yet there has been no in-depth study of Dreux, despite an impressive number of newspaper reports published in the heat of

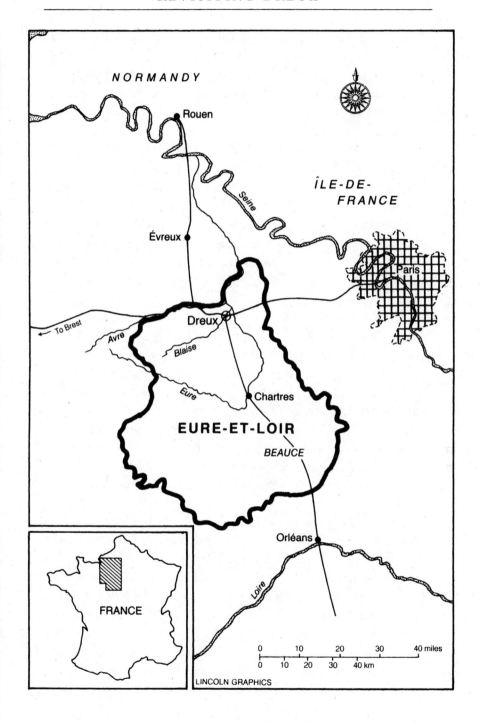

LINCOLN GRAPHICS

events and a large number of editorials treating events in Dreux as symptomatic of the political condition of France as a whole. No political scientist or sociologist has studied the city in order to understand the process that transformed a quiet town rooted in a tradition harking back to the Third Republic (France in the late nineteenth and early twentieth centuries) into a symbol of endangered democracy. Dreux, moreover, is generally described as a "special case." What happened there, we are told, could not have happened anywhere else in France. Dreux is somehow unique.

In 1983, when 16.7 percent of Dreux's voters favored the National Front slate in a local by-election, polling pundits, armed with mysterious knowledge wreathed in mathematics and backed up by high-speed computers, vied to reassure the public that there was nothing to worry about. All the surveys agreed: in France as a whole no more than 2 percent of the electorate favored the extreme right.[3] Although a tiny party like the National Front, which reflected the views of only a small fraction of the voting public, had managed to attract enough votes in Dreux to disturb the calculations of the major national parties, it was attributed to "specific" local reasons: the population of the city included large numbers of immigrants; local political rivalries had created an opening for a new party; and the election in question was a simple by-election in which voters felt free to express their discontent precisely because no major national issues were at stake.

From September 1983 through March 1989, however, the extremist vote in Dreux was overshadowed by the success of the extreme right throughout France. In June 1984 the National Front obtained 11 percent of the vote nationwide, considerably exceeding the 5 percent level required for parliamentary representation. By the time of the 1986 legislative elections, the left had instituted proportional representation, and the National Front's 9.65 percent of the vote was enough to capture 35 seats in the Assembly. Even more impressive, the leader of the extreme right captured 14.4 percent of the vote in the first round of the May 1988 presidential elections, confirming the emergence of a new political force and casting the Dreux results back into the shadows. All across France, in cities from Marseilles to Roubaix to Mulhouse, the National Front outdid its success in Dreux. There was no denying the facts: the vote for the extreme right was a national, not a local, phenomenon.

People soon began to speak of a "conflagration." Everyone invoked the past: as at other times in French history—in 1934 with the Ligues and in 1956 with the Poujadists—an economic crisis had brought about conditions in which right-wing extremism could spread like wildfire. Eventually the flames would subside. Economic growth would take care of things. Historians, demographers, and sociologists produced statistics intended to demonstrate that, worrisome though the cancer might be, it afflicted mainly "problem" cities, those with high levels of immigration. This comforting idea was eagerly accepted, all the more so because the return to majority voting (rather than proportional representation) had virtually eliminated the National Front from the National Assembly in 1988. The Front managed to elect only one deputy, who survived a three-person contest, and the party seemed to have lost its national audience. To make matters worse, the logic of parliamentary politics led the Front's only deputy, Yanne Piat, to affiliate with deputies from the Rassemblement pour la République (RPR), a party of the traditional right. The results of the March 1989 municipal elections seemed to confirm, further, that the National Front's victories came mainly in cities with problems.

In November 1989, however, the world's spotlights once again focused on Dreux, along with Marseilles, when both cities were holding parliamentary by-elections. To the surprise of most observers, the Socialist candidates were eliminated in both places after the first round of voting. In Dreux, the National Front candidate, a woman, was elected in the second round, even though most politicians and political scientists had clung to the belief that, except in the case of a three-way contest, it was impossible for a Front candidate to win a local election.[4]

5

Having failed to predict the scope of the National Front's impact heralded by the Dreux results in 1983, were the commentators more cautious this time around? Did what happened in one district *(circonscription)* in the Eure-et-Loir, confirmed by election results in Marseilles and other places,[5] suggest that the National Front had made progress in its efforts to woo French voters? The experts unanimously responded in the negative. For François Goguel, one of France's leading political scientists, "the role of the personal factor was decisive . . . The fact that the Socialist Party failed to choose Françoise Gaspard as its candidate in Dreux . . . was a miscalculation." For Jérôme Jaffre, a polling expert, the Dreux and Marseilles results proved that these two cities were not typical of France as a whole, for they had been "hotbeds of National Front support since the phenomenon first emerged."[6] Dreux, with its immigrants and internecine political battles, was still seen as atypical, a sort of minor Marseilles north of the Loire.

The analysts also discussed Dreux from the vantage point of Paris. Meanwhile, the public formed an impression of the situation in Dreux on the basis of newspaper and magazine articles, some of them so inaccurate that they even got the statistics wrong.[7] At times it seems as though scholars are afraid to come to Dreux lest they find there an epitome of all the problems facing France in this final decade of the twentieth century. "The Unsavory City of Dreux," read the headline of one weekly newsmagazine after the December 1989 elections.[8] Are we afraid of the truth behind the headlines?

In my case, no pilgrimage to Dreux was necessary. I was born there, my roots go far back, and I have held political office in the city. So I wondered if I might be in a very good position to trace the origins of the present political situation. And I came to the conclusion that I was, since no one else showed any intention of studying the city at first hand. As for my objectivity, there is no such thing as a "pure" historian or sociologist, one without local, regional, philosophical, religious, or political ties. My biases are well known.

Another reason for writing this book was that I read *The Nazi Seizure of Power: The Experience of a Single German Town, 1930–1935* by the American sociologist William Sheridan Allen, and I couldn't get it out of my mind.[9] Allen shows how the Nazi Party little by little created a place for itself in one small German city, a city typical in its own way of Germany as a whole. In 1983 a friend of mine, a socialist activist and teacher in a Dreux high school who had been my classmate at the Institut d'Etudes Politiques in Paris, brought the book, which we had been required to read at school, to my office and laid it on my desk. I reread it. As the years went by, it grew upon me that what was happening in Dreux resembled what had happened in Thalburg in the 1930s.

Of course Dreux is not Thalburg. France in the nineties is not Germany in the thirties. The National Front is not the Nazi Party, and Le Pen is not Hitler. Last but not least, I am not W. S. Allen. But given the size of the National Front vote in the December 1989 elections, I felt the need to revisit Dreux, even if the time was not yet ripe for a full-blown history of the events I had witnessed. Having already dabbled in the history of Dreux in the nineteenth century and the interwar years, I was ready to try my hand again. I reread what the national newspapers had said about Dreux and systematically examined the local press over a period of fifteen years. I took a close look at census data. I analyzed the results of election after election. I established a chronology and charted curves. And then I sat down to write.

What I offer is not an eyewitness account. It would have been artificial and clumsy, however, not to have written certain passages in the first person, when I was involved in events as an observer or a participant. But I did not systematically study my successors in local office. I was reluctant to do so in part because my judgments in such matters are likely to be subjective—but most of all because I am convinced that the role of political figures in these events was secondary at best. What happened in Dreux was shaped primarily by larger economic and social trends, by national policies regarding the regions, and by deep-seated changes in French society.

Nor was my objective to write an essay about the National Front, its ideology and electorate. Instead I wanted to understand what happened in Dreux as the starting point for the rise of the extreme right. I began with the assumption that Dreux is a small French city not unlike many others and that the evolution of events there paralleled events in the rest of the country.

Yet just as history never repeats itself, what happens in one place is never precisely the same as what happens anywhere else: Dreux is Dreux, not Agen or Troyes. Still it will emerge in the course of this study that Dreux is more typical than not. However much my hometown may differ from Agen and Troyes, all three places have in common something at least as important as their differences: they are part of the same national community. The extremist vote is just one of many symptoms of a crisis in French society.

Alfred Grosser's 1967 preface to Allen's book began with the words: "*Wie konnte es geschehen?* How could it happen? The question has repeatedly been asked both inside and outside Germany, especially by young people reaching the age of reason and discovering what Nazism was." The young people who discovered what Nazism was in the 1960s are in positions of responsibility today. In November 1989 they saw the fall of the Berlin wall as marking the end of a century scarred by memories of the Holocaust and the gulags. For some time the old ideologies had been tottering. Socialism and liberalism, to say nothing of Stalinism, Nazism, and fascism, faded into history. Democracy remained. A few weeks later, on 4 December 1989, the generation that had witnessed these changes as it was growing up learned from the headlines that one small city in France had voted massively in favor of a party that carried within it a germ potentially fatal to democracy.

How could it happen?

Intruders in the City

· 1 ·

On the roads leading into Dreux from Paris, Alençon, and Chartres, signs placed at the city limits used to inform visitors of the town's past and local sights: "Dreux, royal city, [with] its church, chapel, belltower, and museum." Not that anyone harbored illusions as to the city's actual interest to tourists: these faded old signs appeared to have been put up for form's sake only. Then at some point the old signs were replaced by new ones. Featuring the royal chapel in the background, the new signs proclaim: "Dreux, Nouveau Visage." This information cannot fail to intrigue the tourist. What "new face" are they talking about? Is it perhaps the face given Dreux by the alliance forged there between political parties of the right and the extreme right in 1983? Since 1984 the magazine published by Dreux's city government has also been entitled "Dreux, Nouveau Visage." Its glossy, full-color cover pictures a man, woman, and child in the city-hall park. The man is in his thirties, tan but not Mediterranean, a typical young executive. His wife is blond and smiling, no doubt a housewife.

The images run together, their outlines blur. So just where is Dreux? The curious tourist will want to "go down into town" (*descendre en ville*), as local people say, because you must travel downhill a way to reach the center of the old town, which is still what people mean when they speak of "the city." To continue the

9

tour, however, you have to climb back uphill toward the outskirts. Along the way it becomes apparent that Dreux is a city composed of overlapping, concentric circles laid down one on top of another like geological strata. Because of a recent geological incident, moreover, an extremely important layer happens to have been deposited on the high plains that encircle the hollow containing the old town, which, having pushed the new stratum aside, has managed to remain intact.

If we are to understand the city and its people, to find out how they think and what they look like, we must subject all these strata to careful examination.

Dreux, Royal City

In the cobblestone streets, stone monuments, and ancient though seemingly solid timber-framed houses of central Dreux, five or six centuries of history are plainly visible. Scratch the soil a little and you will turn up traces of ancient Gauls and Roman roadways, signs that human beings were settled here more than 2,000 years ago, living in the hollow of this valley first in a fortified town and later in a full-fledged city. As recently as a century ago, this historic center was all there was to Dreux.

"Dreux, its church." It is hardly surprising that Dreux has a church—it would be far more surprising if it didn't. Yet Saint-Pierre is not a cathedral, merely a somewhat overelaborate church begun in the thirteenth century and more than five centuries in the making. Nothing about it is particularly striking, unless it is the unfinished southern tower, which lends the whole structure an air of incompleteness somehow bizarrely in harmony with its surroundings.

The belltower, not far from Saint-Pierre, is architecturally very different from the church and worth a detour. It is Dreux's proudest monument, but the tourist guides make little of it. Countless English tourists making their way from Dieppe to southern France bypass Dreux and hasten across the Beauce to Chartres and its cathedral; in doing so they miss an amazing sight. When the bell-tower was built in the sixteenth century, its modernity must have shocked more than one resident of the town. I don't know what impelled the townspeople to raise such an audacious structure. It is easy to imagine the bitter polemics that must have swirled around the construction of this magnificent square tower in the very center of Dreux. It epitomizes the aesthetic conflicts of the time. The first story is flamboyant gothic. The second is in the style known as transitional gothic. The third, in renaissance style, marks an astonishing break with the past. Clément Métezeau, a native of Dreux and the first of a line of important French architects, was one of its designers. But just above the renaissance story, the top of the tower reverts to the gothic—in other words, to what was then a conformist aesthetic. Had the innovators been judged too bold? To today's spectator, however, the tower is an ensemble as harmonious as it is elegant. What is more, a recent restoration has done away with certain improvements that one of Viollet-le-Duc's followers saw fit to inflict upon the monument in the 1870s. It is worth noting that the belltower served as Dreux's city hall for more than three centuries.

Nicolas de Gravelle, the alderman who commissioned the tower, and the many craftsmen who from 1512 on contributed to its construction certainly helped to forge Dreux's identity. Without the belltower, there would be no Grande Rue and, without the Grande Rue, no Dreux. Instinctively one feels that this superb monument is not only beautiful but insolent. Through its bold design, sixteenth-century merchants demonstrated a determination to assert their power in the face of royal authority. In those days the bourgeoisie's message had something of a revolutionary tenor, and the local branches of left-wing political parties have often taken Dreux's belltower as their emblem.

"Dreux, royal city." It was not the only one. Other royal residences included Anet, a fortified town in the northern part of the district with a castle that is a renaissance jewel, and cities of the Loire, somewhat farther south. But Dreux is more entitled to the appellation than any of its rivals. In 911 King Charles III signed the treaty of Saint-Clair-sur-Epte in the hope of ending Viking incursions into the kingdom of France. Under the terms of the treaty, Normandy was ceded to the Normans while Dreux remained French. Dreux was thus a border town, a fortified city overlooking the plains of Rollo's Normandy and the gateway to the kingdom. After becoming a royal estate, it was given symbolically to the king's brother as part of his appanage. But the price of the treaty signed by Charles III—also known as Charles the Simple—turned out to be exorbitant. Over the next three centuries Dreux was constantly embattled. Blood ran in the streets at times, and the people of Dreux endured the ravages of repeated sieges intended to starve them into submission. Peace was not restored until Philippe Auguste carried the day at Château-Gaillard in 1204, and even then it lasted no more than a century.

The royal family remained loyal to Dreux, vigilant gatekeeper of its kingdom. The Duc de Penthièvre, one of Louis XIV's legitimated bastards and, on the eve of the revolution, the last man to hold the title of Comte de Dreux, loved the city. He chose the collegiate church of Saint-Etienne in Dreux as his family's burial place and expressed his wish to be buried there himself. His daughter Marie-Adélaïde, wife of Philippe Egalité, returned from exile in 1814 to pray at the graves of her ancestors only to find the tombs violated and the remains scattered. Within the walls of the old medieval castle she started to construct a new burial vault. In 1816, accompanied by her son, the future king Louis Philippe, she laid the first stone of the royal chapel of Dreux, where the dead of the Orleanist line have ever since been buried, close to the citizen king. In a sense I owe it to Marie-Adélaïde that I was born in Dreux. An ancestor on my father's side was a stonecutter who toured France in his apprentice years and settled in Dreux, the story goes, when the Orléans family hired him to rough out sculptures intended to embellish their tombs. He settled not far from the chapel in the house I grew up in. In 1869 his son went into business as a marble mason, and today, five generations later, my brother carries on the family tradition.

To the residents of Dreux, the rather peculiar chapel built by Lefranc, with its huge dome that seems to bubble up out of the earth, is a familiar fixture of the landscape. Since it stands on high ground, it is impossible to miss. If you happen to be walking down the Grande Rue, you have only to turn your back to the belltower and there is the chapel, looming large on the horizon. Yet the people of Dreux proudly ignore it, resolutely turning up their noses at the city's royal heritage. The Comte de Paris (present-day pretender to the throne) frequently complains of this antiroyalist sentiment, deploring the fact that none of his efforts to develop the royal domain have borne fruit. To this day his daughter-in-law and grandsons inhabit a rambling building flanked by towers that overlooks the center of town, but no one pays them any heed. The only Drouais who notice that the pretender's heir-apparent lives among them are those who happen to pick up a copy of *Jours de France* while waiting at the dentist's office or the hairdresser's.

So the city has its church, its belltower, and its royal chapel. I almost forgot to mention the museum, where as a child I was fascinated not so much by Monet's *Wisteria* (actually a study) as by a small collection of Merovingian weapons. In short, Dreux is like many other small French cities. It boasts a few handsome buildings. One of them is the subprefecture office, which people would rather not recall used to be occupied by a future president of the Republic, whose administrative career began here: unfortunately Paul Deschanel has become a figure of jest, since all that most people remember about him is that he once fell from a train in his pyjamas. There is also a courthouse, an ordinary district court. The city hall, having been removed from the belltower to a more convenient new building, is now located in what was once the home of Madame Coche, a baroness of prerevolutionary lineage and the last of the local aristocracy, who acquired her *hôtel particulier* from the counts of Arjuson, wealthy landlords with estates in the surrounding countryside. Today the mayor of Dreux sits in an armchair set in front of the fireplace in what used to be the grand salon of this noble residence. I remember seeing the Baroness Coche de la Ferté from the windows of my grandparents' house, which overlooked the grounds of her estate. In the summer the servants carried the elderly woman about in a wicker sedan chair. In that way she was able to take the sun on the lawn where, after I was elected mayor, I sometimes took visitors out for a stroll.

Druids, Durocassians, Drouais

The signs indicating Dreux's principal sights evoked the city's old fortunes but not its remote past. The church, the belltower, and the royal chapel belong to the last five centuries of Dreux's history, but the city's origins are far more ancient.

"Autrefois notre pays s'appelait la Gaule et les habitants s'appellaient les Gaulois" (Long ago our country was called Gaul, and its inhabitants were called Gauls). Many people still living in France today once learned this sentence by heart: it was the opening line of a lesson in what used to be the standard history textbook in French schools, the "Petit Lavisse," as it was affectionately known after the name of its editor, Ernest Lavisse. If the Gauls were the ancestors of the French, then Dreux stands at the heart of that mythical nation sanctified by the textbooks of the Third Republic. Until the end of the nineteenth century, inhabitants of Dreux held the unshakable belief that their city had been the Druid capital and owed its name to the Druids. In 1821 Victor Hugo, writing from Dreux to Alfred de Vigny, expressed surprise that there was no Druid monument in the city or the surrounding countryside. "Dreux," he went on, "gave its name to the Druids."[1] It is said that the forest around Dreux was a place where Druids from the land of the Carnutes settled, but there is no proof of this. When I was a child, a ritual was still celebrated at a place known as "Saint Louis' oak." Oddly enough, the story behind this linked Saint Louis with secret Druid ceremonies. Can the ritual be traced back, as one local historian claims, to the time of the Gauls? The story is not very plausible.

The Frankish kings attempted to bolster their legitimacy by spreading the idea that the people of the kingdom were of the same "race" as themselves. Royal historians magnified the grandeur of that race by tracing its origin back to Troy. This founding myth of Frankish grandeur flourished until the end of the middle ages. It is hard to believe that the inhabitants of Dreux would have resisted the ambient culture for centuries by cultivating a Druid memory that the rest of France had rejected. In any case, the Druids vanished from Gaul during the reign of Emperor Claudius in the first century, leaving no written trace of their presence. The fact remains that the people of Dreux used the similarity between the name of their town and that of the Druids to invent a tradition, to rediscover the Druids and the Gauls. No one knows when this happened. What we do know is that certain fifteenth-century chroniclers in search of their roots claimed that Dreux had been built by the Gauls, which is true, and that it had been the capital of the Druids, which is pure fiction. "When a nation becomes conscious of its existence, it tries to account for its present in terms of its past. In this sense it was historians who created the nation." After quoting these words of Jacques Guénée, Jacques Rossiaud adds: "This observation is also applicable to that fatherland within a fatherland, the city: without history there would be no cities."[2] In the early modern period, in other words, Dreux fabricated its own past in order to stake out its identity.

In the nineteenth century, historians armed with old Roman maps attempted to put things right: the etymology of the name Dreux, in spite of appearances, had nothing to do with the master magicians of ancient Gaul. In fact, Dreux was called Durocassium in Roman times, a name purportedly derived from Duro Cath, meaning "river fortress" in the language of the Celts. Celtic tribes from the north had allegedly settled in the surrounding countryside five centuries before the birth of Christ. If Dreux took its name from the Celtic, the residents would be well advised to stop calling themselves Druids and adopt the name Durocassians instead. But the fancy appellation proposed by the scholars never caught on, and its only effect was to put an end to invocations of the Druids.

Today the residents of Dreux refer to themselves, conventionally enough, as Drouais. The legend and its associated memories, the myth and the history, have been forgotten. Dreux no longer stakes any claim to Gallic origins or a romanized Celtic name. It has no memory of having been rescued, along with the rest of Gaul, from its German occupiers by Julius Caesar. In any case, the Durocassians, unlike their neighbors the Carnutes, reputedly put up little resistance against their conquerors. Caesar camped on the site where the city now stands. The Romans built roads that outlined the town and facilitated its development. Excavations still turn up Roman coins from the age of the Antonines, evidence that a prosperous town existed here in the second century.

The Romans were not the last foreigners to occupy the region. Germans employed as Roman mercenaries most likely camped in the vicinity of Dreux in the fourth century. Later, Vandals probably passed through the area some time before the Franks overran the entire territory. Still later, the Vikings tried to establish a foothold. Their invasion in 889 was far from peaceful—certainly far less peaceful than the twentieth-century invasion of workers in search of jobs. After failing to capture Paris, the Vikings sacked and burned the city of Dreux. Like the Romans, Germans, and other invaders, they surely left offspring behind. By the dawn of the second millennium, "our ancestors the Gauls" were a distant memory, and the local race had mingled its blood with that of countless foreigners.

Dreux was repeatedly fought over, invaded, and conquered. Less well known is the city's deep involvement in the first Franco-French wars of early modern times. In 1407 the murder of Louis of Orléans on the streets of Paris after his brother Charles VI granted him the county of Dreux sparked what would become the war between the Armagnacs and the Burgundians. The duke of

Burgundy, John the Fearless, had armed Louis' murderer. Louis' son took refuge in Dreux. To avenge his father he employed mercenaries in the service of his father-in-law, the count of Armagnac. In the ensuing war, Dreux was not free to choose sides: its prince had placed it in the Armagnac camp. In 1412 the town came under Burgundian fire. For four days the Burgundians shelled the ramparts, then entered and sacked the city.

Two and a half centuries later, Dreux was the site of a sinister battle that inaugurated thirty years of religious war. Tempers had been running high since 1562, between Catholics and Huguenots (Protestants). The regent, Catherine de Médicis, tried in vain to restore peace between the two camps, with the royal court itself divided. On 1 March the Duc de Guise, leader of the Catholic party, encountered a group of Protestants. The ensuing scuffle turned into a slaughter (the so-called massacre of Wassy), and from then on there was no turning back: the dead had to be avenged. A few months later the prince of Condé, a Calvinist, occupied Orléans with his troops. He was determined to link up with English forces in Rouen. At stake was no longer only the civil peace but the integrity of the kingdom. The regent sent the royal army to intercept the Protestant army. On 18 December the Catholics Montmorency and Guise spent the night at the castle of Mézières, a short way from Dreux. All that remains today of that vast fortress is a portion of a tower, which as it happens forms one corner of the little house in which I am writing these pages. The Protestant army, led by Admiral de Coligny and the prince of Condé, had set up camp one league away. On the following day the battle began. The outcome hung in the balance for so long that Catherine, who was following developments from Rambouillet, resigned herself to what seemed an inevitable Protestant victory: "Oh, well!" she sighed in the presence of Brantôme, "Too bad! We shall have to hear the mass in French." But Guise's triumphant arrival that very night filled Catholic hearts with joy: mass would be said in Latin after all. Condé was taken prisoner. He slept under heavy guard on the outskirts of Dreux, while in the meantime, on the battlefield, eight thousand men met their deaths. Every year until the revolution of 1789, Dreux honored the victors in that struggle with a huge commemorative procession.

It would be helpful to know more about life in Dreux during the ancien régime. But apart from recent times, the only historians who have been interested in the city were self-taught natives with distinct biases. Their works are as incomplete as they are one-sided. The celebration of the bicentennial of the French revolution might have shed some light on local history in the years preceding the great upheaval that ushered in the modern age. In 1988 the mayor assigned responsibility for bicentennial planning to his cultural assistant, a member of the National Front. With the aid of a committee she chose "revolutionary vandalism" as a theme for the commemoration. It is a pity that this subject, selected for obvious ideological reasons, failed to inspire the local historians, some of whom are very good scholars. In fact, on 20 July 1789, the people of Dreux captured their own Bastille: the Maison des Aydes, headquarters of the local tax collector. It would have been instructive to explore the particulars of this event. It also would have been interesting to know the reasons for the revolutionaries' zeal in attacking the tympanum above the church door with hammers. What caused their rage? How had the clergy behaved before the abolition of their privileges? And though a good deal is known about the activities of the local People's Society during the Terror, it would be interesting to find out who purchased confiscated national properties during that period. Thus it might be possible to understand how power was redistributed in the city in the nineteenth century. The fortunes in land amassed at that time might explain some of the political divisions in the city today.

Streets, Cemeteries, Monuments

The memory of those centuries and of the people who made history lives on in the names of the city's streets. Like most children who grow up in a fairly small town, I walked those streets every day. I liked to take different routes to school. I walked from my parents' house to my grandparents' and on Thursdays to the municipal library and the Cercle Laïque. Those streets were an education. I had no idea how streets get their names. I had no notion that street names are a political prize and that the choice of a name reveals the political hue of the city council that approved it. I didn't learn this lesson until much later, when, as mayor myself, I had to baptize new streets.

The Place Rotrou, rue Rotrou, and the Lycée Rotrou all honor the most illustrious of Dreux's native sons. When I attended the Sorbonne, I was chagrined to discover that most of my fellow students had no idea who Jean de Rotrou was. Even during his lifetime he was already overshadowed by Corneille. Still he managed to write thirty-five successful verse plays, before meeting his death in the line of duty at the age of forty-one. As the *lieutenant civil et criminel*—something like the sheriff—for the *baillage* of Dreux, he hastened to the city from Paris in June 1650 upon learning that his fellow citizens were threatened by an outbreak of plague. He spoke of the situation in a letter to friends: "Not that the danger where I am is not great, for even as I write the bells are tolling for the twenty-second person to die today. My turn may come tomorrow, but my conscience has shown me where my duty lies. May God's will be done."[3] He died three days later. Rotrou thus figured in my civic as well as my literary education, and each time I pass his statue I pay my respects.

General de Billy gave his name to the street I grew up on. At age ten I knew every detail of the life of this scion of a local family of pewterers. A friend of Marceau and Kléber, he made a name for himself in Napoleon's imperial army before falling at Auerstedt in 1806. The story of his death was as familiar to me as if I had heard it from the lips of a grizzled veteran. By contrast, I felt no sympathy for Antoine Godeau when I walked the street that bears his name, and I am indulgent toward those who are unaware that he was once bishop of Grasse and Vence and became—through intrigue, people say—one of the first members of the Académie

Française. Last but not least, only a select few music lovers and avid chessplayers have heard of François-André Danican Philidor. Every day I passed the house in which he was born, and I imagined myself a visitor there early in the eighteenth century while the young page from Louis XV's chapel played one of his own compositions. So much for Dreux's celebrities.

To find out about other people who lived in Dreux, one has to visit the town cemetery. Their suffering, happiness, pride, and humility can be read on their tombstones, the city's silent memorial. The city council balked in 1985 when I tried to use the regulations governing cemeteries to prevent the "recovery" of abandoned graves without regard for local history (recovery was the official term for the practice of reusing old graves after quietly removing the remains). I wanted to stop the excavation of the oldest section of Dreux's cemetery. As it happened, the people buried there were not obscure, hard-working laborers. The cemetery was no different from the city itself: it had its "good sections" where space cost more and cost was determined by duration. The paupers buried in potter's field were forgotten in a few years. Families of modest means could purchase a thirty-year concession, and the lease could be renewed. As one rose to higher levels of the social hierarchy, the concession was extended to fifty or a hundred years. More recently the very wealthy were allowed to purchase perpetual concessions. But as the city grew, the dead became a burden. Eternity could no longer be bought at any price. After thirty, fifty, or a hundred years the city has the right to recover a person's grave. The marker and remains are removed and the hole reverts to the city, which can then sell it to someone else. If the authorities are not vigilant, irreplaceable vestiges of the past will be lost.

The section of Dreux's cemetery with the perpetual graves, where the city's most illustrious personages are buried, is also the oldest. Those with an ancient lineage, an established fortune, or public renown felt obliged to build burial vaults commensurate with their status. The inscriptions on these tombs tell the story of over two centuries of Dreux's political and social history. The names that appear come up in local history well before the beginning of the nineteenth century. "A few allied family dynasties permanently presided over the fate of Marseilles, Lyons, and most other cities," Fernand Braudel wrote of France under the ancien régime.[4] And so it was with Dreux. In the cemetery the same names appear repeatedly and in various combinations on the more impressive monuments and vaults. Some of them are the same names that appear on the street signs. Over the years, though, vaults have fallen into ruin, stone structures have crumbled, and moss and weeds have taken over. The Rotrous, Lamésanges, Gromards, Dubois—the former mayors and other people of privilege who for centuries dominated the city—seem to have stopped reproducing. What became of those dynasties that Braudel called permanent?

Monuments to the dead are no less instructive. Dreux paid its tribute of soldiers in all of France's wars, from the monarchy to the revolution to the First Empire: for every General de Billy, who gave his name to a street in Dreux and a quay in Paris, how many imperial troopers from Dreux fell at Jena, Austerlitz, and Waterloo? No one knows. Nor does anyone know who from Dreux went to Crimea or Mexico under the Second Empire, never to return. The commemoration of those who "died on the field of honor," the municipal monuments raised in every town, began only after a national consciousness had emerged, that is, after France developed a nationalist ideology. Thus the first monuments to the dead, in honor of those who fell in the Franco-Prussian war of 1870–71, were built, according to Antoine Prost, at the end of the nineteenth century: "They were built not in the emotional period of national mourning but twenty or thirty years later, after the Boulangist episode and at the turn of the twentieth century, when the Republic seemed to turn its eyes away from the blue line of the Vosges."[5]

Witnesses to the history of contemporary France, these monuments were controversial at first but later became pilgrimage sites.

This sanctification of France's war dead explains the proliferation of monuments to the dead in Dreux. Instead of a single monument, there are four different ones: one for the Franco-Prussian war; one dedicated to those who died in the Great War, the 1939–1945 campaign, Indochina, and Algeria; one for those deported by the Germans during World War II; and another for local residents shot by the Germans.

Most people in Dreux are not even aware of the existence of the Franco-Prussian war memorial. In the long procession that moves from monument to monument and tomb to tomb on Armistice Day (11 November), politicians and veterans make their way across the municipal cemetery, stopping first at the square honoring British aviators before moving on to the stele commemorating Dreux's deportees. But they do not stop in front of the obelisk bearing this sober, lapidary inscription: "To the French soldiers killed outside its walls, 1870–71, the city of Dreux." One war supplants another in popular memory, and generations vanish into oblivion. But sometimes forgetfulness is the result of a deliberate decision or choice. The 1870 monument marks a moment when the city was divided, and it is hard to cast the events of that era in a glorious light. In October 1870 the elected officials of Dreux did not resist the Prussians. Believing their forces to be insufficient and skeptical of the success of the massive conscription called for by Gambetta, they ordered the evacuation of reinforcements rushed in from Normandy, disarmed the National Guard, and declared Dreux an open city in order to avoid the kind of shelling that the Germans had inflicted on fortified towns that resisted their advance. When valiant patriots nevertheless decided to try and stop the enemy, there were some accidental deaths: the defenders inadvertently fired on other local partisans. Given this history, it is difficult to make a speech about local heroism without reawakening old divisions between those who wanted to fight and those who did not. Memories of the controversies that agitated the city at the time of the Third Republic's inception and of the debates that erupted when contributions were solicited for the building of the monument a century ago remain more acute than one might think.

As for the three other monuments intended to remind the living of the sacrifices made by their fellow Drouais, each has its own history. The families of those who died after being deported to Germany wanted a separate memorial in their honor. In 1982 the Communists commissioned a stele in another location to honor young Dreux Communists shot by the Germans in Nantes and Amiens and on Mont Valérien. The oldest of the three monuments, the one honoring those who fell in the Great War, was built in 1920 with contributions collected by veterans—men whom the mayor considered to be rank conservatives. Over time, however, this monument gained acceptance as the city's official memorial, and the names of those who had died in the "war to end all wars" were eventually joined by others who fell in Morocco, in the struggle against the Nazis, and in Indochina and Algeria. The once-controversial monument is now universally respected. Each newly elected mayor lays a wreath at the spot. When a new subprefect is appointed, he or she makes a first public appearance there. On national holidays squads of veterans, impressively numerous in the 1950s but nowadays rather sparse, converge on the spot. In the past the participants in these ceremonies marched from monument to monument on foot; now they ride in buses. City officials pay homage to the dead at each place on the appropriate date, being sure not to forget the plaque at the railway station commemorating the sacrifices made by railway workers in the Resistance. Sometimes these commemorative ceremonies are disrupted by demonstrators: a group of pacifists may seek a public hearing or a party may try to capture the headlines by laying its own wreath, thus ruining one of the few occasions on which the citizens of troubled Dreux might come together in harmony.

Markets and Fairs

Let us turn now from the dead to the living—who found themselves embroiled in a considerable controversy over the Monday market. When I was elected mayor in 1977, I proposed bringing this weekly street market back into the center of town, at the foot of the belltower; my predecessors had sent it farther out because it interfered with traffic. Traditionally the market was held in the center of town, as I remembered from childhood. The creation of a downtown pedestrian zone paved the way for moving the market back to its traditional site. The move was made not so much for nostalgic reasons as to restore life to a dying city center, but I confess that I was also pleased personally by the change, for the market—which my successors have again moved away from the center—loomed large in the memory of every native of Dreux. Something important had happened to just about every one of us there. Take a story told by an old friend of my grandmother's, a woman who passed away in 1990 in her one-hundredth year. On 11 November 1918 the sun shone brightly as she, along with other young women of the town, awaited news of the war's impending end. She was in the market that morning, selling eggs and chickens in little baskets on rue Rotrou, when at 11 o'clock the bells began to ring. The war was over—her fiancé, a colonel, would be coming home.

It was in this market that my ancestors sold their animals and grain. They gathered in the market-shed café (both shed and café are now gone) to discuss the price of a bushel of grain or the cost of renting an acre of land. I can imagine them returning on foot or by cart to the village where my mother's family had lived since the fifteenth century. The road they would have taken was known locally as "Last Cent Way," a name taken from an inn where men on their way home stopped for a drink and sometimes wound up spending every last cent they had made at the fair. Today the inn is a private home, but the old sign is still visible. My grandmother tells me that the women in my family used to curse this den of iniquity. Whenever she spoke of it, her voice betrayed a sense of shame and anger no doubt inherited from her mother, who in turn took it from her mother, and so on as far back as anyone can remember. The women couldn't go to market because someone had to stay home to milk the cows, and they shuddered to think that the men of the house might drink up all their earnings. I suppose that the name of my ancestral village, well known to crossword puzzle addicts throughout France, might originally have had something to do with the homecomings of these bibulous men: the place is called Bû (a homonym of *bu*, the past participle of the verb *boire*, to drink).

Several times a year, Dreux's Monday market grew into a large fair. The two most important fairs were held in the fall, after the harvest was in: the Saint-Gilles in September and the Saint-Denis in October. Although some farmers brought animals to sell, most came to spend money. The Saint-Denis fair dates back almost a thousand years: in 1180 Robert I granted the local Friars Hospitaler the right to hold a fair. It is the only fair still held in Dreux today, but without the animals, especially the thousands of sheep which as recently as the nineteenth century made fair days such picturesque occasions. Here is an eyewitness account of one such day late in the last century: "Flocks of sheep make their way down through the Saint-Martin district on the heights. Horses, their tails and manes festooned with straw, prance in the Vieux-Pré under the watchful eye of the auctioneers. Country folk dressed to the nines expertly appraise hundreds of cows and hogs. Broken-down wagons and carts line the streets around inns on the city's periphery."[6]

The Monday market, a fixture of Dreux life for ten centuries, was part of the local culture. There town and country met and mingled. News was exchanged, and rumors too. Today the "opinion of the marketplace" in fact reflects the views of old Dreux and its surrounding villages, and television cameras often follow the candidates at election time as they make their obligatory swing through Dreux's street fair.

The War

The War and the Occupation: for Dreux as for many other small French cities, the period from 1940 to 1944 was truly a time of sorrow and pity, to borrow from the title of the well-known film.

The shelling and bombardment of the city on 9 and 10 June 1940 killed many residents and sent others into panicked flight, joining people from Belgium and northern France already clogging the roads leading south. Jean Moulin, the prefect of Eure-et-Loir, was one of the few government officials to remain at his post during the debacle.[7] On 14 June he visited the mayor of Dreux, Maurice Viollette, and inspected the city, which lay in ruins. Of that visit he wrote: "I looked at Viollette, seated beside me. Tomorrow, perhaps within a few hours, his city was to be surrendered to the enemy, a city that for thirty years he had led, at times in rather rough fashion. In it there is not one neighborhood, one street, one patch of earth that does not owe something to his efforts. His adversaries say that he suffered from 'construction fever.' And it's true. He built endlessly: hospitals, kindergartens, sanatoriums, workers' housing . . . As we drive through streets strewn with ruins, it occurs to me that it is not such a bad thing to be labeled a 'builder.' "[8] Two days later, when the Germans entered Dreux, barely 600 of the 13,000 people who had been living there a few weeks before still remained.[9]

Maurice Viollette was thirty-eight years old when he became mayor. He had served as deputy for the district since 1902. A young lawyer who once headed the staff of Alexandre Millerand, he chose not to join the Section Française de l'Internationale Ouvrière (SFIO) when it was created in 1905. Instead he became an independent socialist. By virtue of his background and training he was convinced that most social issues were best resolved on the municipal level. His first actions as mayor were dictated by his fervent anticlericalism: he issued regulations governing the ringing of bells and banning religious processions. Then he embarked on an energetic program to modernize his small city. He set up occupational training courses to promote employment. He built day-care centers, schools, hospitals, and low-cost housing. In 1922 Dreux became one of the first cities in France to open an office to help people find affordable housing. But Viollette wanted no part of barracks-like public housing. Instead of apartments, Dreux built individual houses for working-class families: houses, it was believed, would provide a healthier environment, and having yards to tend at home would keep men from drinking at the local bar. The city grew. It expanded onto the slopes of the valley leading to the plain above. New apartment buildings went up, arrayed around central courtyards with basins in which children could sail their boats. Ample public parks were dotted with replicas of classical statues intended to foster a taste for art. Public schools, reflecting the latest architectural trends, looked out on well-manicured squares and parks.

In 1940 Viollette, who had served briefly as minister of supply during World War I, as governor-general of Algeria from 1925 to 1927, and as vice-president of the council of ministers under Léon Blum during the Popular Front, was no longer a member of the National Assembly. In 1938 he suffered one of the few election defeats of a long political career.[10] The *grands électeurs* of the Beauce made him pay for his participation in the Popular Front and above all for his opposition to the Munich accords of 1938. Hence he was not present at Vichy on 10 July 1940, when a majority of the parliament voted to accord full powers to Marshal Pétain. How would he have voted? "Obviously if I had been in Vichy I would have refused to vote for Pétain, and I would have used all the strength at my disposal to fight against him."[11] His consistent devotion to the Republic strongly suggests that he would have joined the "eighty" who refused to give Pétain the vote of confidence he wanted, which in reality amounted to signing the death warrant of the Third Republic. The diary Viollette kept at the time confirms his opposition.

As long as Jean Moulin remained the prefect of the département, Viollette could quietly oppose the "new order" without interference. The two men were old friends. Under the Popular Front Moulin had been on the staff of Pierre Cot, the minister of aviation. Both Cot and Viollette had favored France's intervention in the Spanish civil war, and Moulin was assigned the task of discreetly arranging for aircraft to be transferred into the hands of the Spanish republicans. The prefect in Chartres and the mayor in Dreux thus shared the same attitude toward the occupying forces and the "French State" (as the Pétain government in Vichy was officially dubbed). Both mounted passive resistance to Vichy's orders and to those of the Germans. In November Moulin was removed from his post, and in December Viollette was dismissed. The new prefect named one of Viollette's right-wing adversaries, a Dreux attorney, as acting mayor. A month later, the acting mayor had Viollette arrested in the name of the French State: "In view of the fact that his presence in the city and the département in which he has held elective office is apt, under present circumstances, to incite an agitation dangerous to national defense and public security," Viollette was placed under house arrest in Ille-et-Vilaine and later in Paris. In the final months of the war, he managed to elude Vichy's surveillance and hide out on a farm not far from Dreux.

Starting in July 1940, the residents of Dreux began returning home, where they had to learn to live on German terms. Not everyone found the new situation tolerable. To mark the first Christmas after the fall of France, the occupying forces erected a Christmas tree on the Grande Rue. On the night of 25 December, someone hung a rabbit skin from the top of the tree. This little joke was credited to the same people who splattered Nazi posters with ink and cut electric wires. These early *résistants* could be counted on the fingers of one hand. Later their numbers were slightly increased by men who refused to obey Nazi orders to leave home and work in Germany under the Compulsory Labor Service. Together they formed a small band of resistance fighters led by one "Mathurin," the pseudonym adopted by Francis Dablin, a gym teacher at the Lycée Rotrou in Dreux.

So much for the sorrow. Pity must be extended to the large numbers of Pétainists and opportunistic collaborators, to all those who quite simply turned whichever way the wind was blowing. After the city's liberation, they became more Gaullist than the Gaullists of 1940.

After the war Mathurin ran a camp—this one quite peaceful—

where his erstwhile wartime comrades, now far too busy with postwar reconstruction to take vacations, could send their children. I was among them. On a beach in Normandy still bearing the scars of the June 1944 landings, we spent our evenings listening eagerly to Mathurin's stories. I was all the more attentive because my father figured in them as a young hero. Today he is one of the last survivors of the Resistance demolition of the Chérisy viaduct. Like everyone who was twenty-five in 1944, the Liberation obliged him to relearn peacetime etiquette. He had to get along with neighbors who a few months earlier had denounced his parents to the Gestapo. He still has in his possession one such letter of denunciation, found in the German police archives, along with a citation awarded to his own father and bearing General Eisenhower's signature. When journalists questioned my father about the most spectacular exploit of the local resistance, his response reflected the feelings of others who shared his experience: "What we did was quite modest. Dreux was not the Vercors."[12] But he has by no means forgotten the past. Even today, when he hears the name of X and Y, he is likely to say, in the present tense, "That one is a *collabo*." There he lets the matter rest.

Life Goes On

After the Liberation, which in Dreux happened on 16 August 1944, life returned to normal. Viollette came home a hero. The Americans handed out chewing gum and chocolate. They brought the medicine that would save my mother's life when I was born in the spring of 1945. The winter of 1944–45 was a harsh one, all the harder to bear because the war was supposed to be over.

In the late 1940s everyone in Dreux knew everyone else. Political views were an open book. Everyone knew who did or did not believe in Radicalism, the local religion (referring not to radicalism as Americans would know it but to the rather centrist politics of the Radical Party). Old divisions reasserted themselves. Pierre Joseph, a socialist and printer who had turned out false identity cards during the Occupation, resumed publication of the *Populaire d'Eure-et-Loir,* a "socialist and feminist weekly" he had scuttled in June 1940. He used to march up and down the Grande Rue wearing a broadbrimmed black hat and a lavaliere around his neck. Charles Maillier, an accountant and local historian as well as a Christian Democrat and adversary of Mayor Viollette, also wore a lavaliere but with a less bohemian hat. Roger Hieaux, a banker and the former regional president of the Croix-de-Feu (a right-wing nationalist group of the 1930s), could be seen late in the afternoon running with his tennis racket toward the municipal courts. Charles Vannier, schoolteacher and communist, walked the Grande Rue, *L'Humanité* under his arm, chatting with the owner of the local hardware store or with a worker from the Potez plant who had come into town at the end of the day for a game of billiards in the backroom of the Café de l'Epoque. Everyone greeted the mayor's assistants, Haricot, Faucher, Le Moullec, and Sébille—names that today's residents of Dreux know only from some municipal housing project or street. The five men together had a combined age of four centuries. They were respected not only for their age but for their constant concern and courtesy.

Though Dreux is a republican city, there are a few misplaced royalists. You have to be an oldtimer, as I am, to remember the shouts of "Long live the king" that echoed one Sunday morning in the early 1950s along the avenue of chestnut trees leading up to the royal estate. Back then, when such greetings for the Comte de Paris on his way to attend mass in his private chapel used to disgust my young republican soul, our family doctor, Henri Monégier du Sorbier, a candidate in the cantonal elections, did not bother to hide his Bonapartist views. Dreux was more than just a textbook in the history of France. Local elections were living illustrations of a textbook in civics or political science, exhibiting all the diversity of the French political scene.

While Dreux's wealthier citizens liked to play tennis, the town's merchants and workingmen were enthusiasts of boxing, soccer, or belote. Children went either to the nondenominational public schools or to the Catholic private school. For cultural activities they turned to the (nondenominational) Cercle Laïque or the (Catholic) Patronage Saint-Jean. For gymnastics they went to the Espérance or the Alliance. Tell me what school you go to and I will tell you who you are. Tell me where you spend your Thursdays and I will tell you how your parents vote. The old order should not be idealized: it was not notable for stability, social harmony, or political serenity. Its social conflicts and election battles were sometimes crude. But public life on the local level did have a reassuring clarity. On one side were the bosses, on the other side the workers; on one side the Catholics, on the other side the anticlericals; on one side the right, on the other side the left. Of course there were some left-wing bosses, some right-wing workers, and some young Catholics who belonged to the fellow-traveling Jeunesse Ouvrière Catholique (Catholic Working Youth), but these were the exceptions that proved the rule.

During the years of postwar reconstruction, which no one at the time suspected marked the beginning of the three decades of unprecedented growth that Jean Fourastié would later name the "Thirty Glorious Years," Dreux's inevitable evolution from a large town to a small city appeared to be a manageable process. In fact, a new Dreux was being born, a birth of which the old citizens of the town were mostly unaware. To be sure, they saw the vestiges of what had been the city of their youth slowly disappearing. They watched the demolition crews raze the old Hôtel du Paradis at the corner of rue aux Tanneurs and the Grande Rue, where Victor Hugo had slept in 1821. In its place a large discount department store moved into a new concrete building that resembled a blockhouse. A few years later, another local landmark even more intimately associated with local life also disappeared: the Café du Commerce was sold, razed, and replaced by a bank with a windowless concrete facade. The people of Dreux were dismayed. The Grande Rue, they said, would never be the same. In a sense, the razing of the Café du Commerce marked Dreux's transition from one kind of city to another. It symbolized a rupture: can one imagine any French city without its Café du Commerce? This one in particular was worthy of its name. It stood in the heart of town and served as an exchange for information of all kinds. It was a forum for political debate, a place where people talked and argued and insisted they had the solutions to the country's problems. A scriptwriter looking for the popular idiom of the day would have found this an ideal place to do research. Of course there were other neighborhood cafés where a businessman could have a cup of coffee before opening up in the morning or an apéritif after closing down at night. But the Café du Commerce was one of a kind.

For the people of Dreux there was solace for this loss in all the unmistakable signs of Dreux's modernization. The installation of the first traffic light was evidence that Dreux had become a genuine city. Townspeople went in large numbers to gawk at the spectacle, just as they did later when the first high-rise building—with an elevator, no less—went up in the center of town, vying with the belltower for the honor of being the tallest structure in Dreux. Yet while the Drouai's were torn between nostalgia for their old town and pride at seeing things in Dreux that had once existed only in Paris, they failed to appreciate the magnitude of the change taking place on the outskirts of the city. The heights were being urbanized and populated by newcomers—but from the center of town these developments were invisible.

One Economy Dies, Another Is Born

The break in Dreux's history is marked not so much by the war, the defeat, and the occupation as by the three decades that followed the restoration of peace. Industrial change was the root cause of a profound upheaval. At the turn of the twentieth century Dreux was not, as has often been said, a large but essentially rural town. Prefects and subprefects were frequently invited to speak at groundbreaking ceremonies, and there was no shortage of opportunities. Invariably, in their bombastic way, they hailed the changes that were transforming the face of this subprefecture: "Dreux, this modest rural town at the gateway of the Beauce, has, thanks to the enterprising spirit of its city fathers, developed into a small but dynamic and well-run industrial city." Countless speeches hailed the transformation of the modest rural town into a small industrial city. When the first signs of crisis cropped up in Dreux, many commentators blamed the problems on the difficulty of making the transition from an agricultural to an industrial economy. As recently as 1990, a program on one of the major television networks invoked that same stereotype.[13]

It is impossible to overemphasize how wrong this theory is. To be sure, Dreux was once an important agricultural market town, and crafts dependent on agriculture (such as milling, tanning, and coopering) were an important element of the city's economy. But Dreux had long been a factory town. As far back as the seventeenth century, a textile plant employed 3,000 people from the town and surrounding villages. Metalworking factories were numerous along the rivers. The paper mill and printing plant built by the Firmin-Didot family at Mesnil-sur-l'Estrée, about six miles outside Dreux, had provided work for local people since the 1600s.

Throughout the nineteenth century, moreover, and again during the period between the two world wars, Dreux was seen as the most industrialized (and most working-class) city in the département. Over the centuries there were, to be sure, painful changes in the local economy. Vineyards disappeared from what had once been a winemaking region. The free-trade agreement of 1860 completed the ruin of a textile industry already in crisis. And there were repeated industrial revolutions. But new businesses moved in to take the place of dying firms, availing themselves of the region's long industrial tradition and plentiful supply of workers.

Only faint traces remain of the economy of the past. The Esmery-Caron jute business was able to grow by diversifying its activities and thus survives as the last vestige of a local textile industry whose roots go back more than three centuries. Overcoming a long series of difficulties, the Firmin-Didot printing plant was saved from shutting down in the 1980s: its ancient presses were scrapped and workers were laid off. Today 190 employees can do the work of 600 in an ultramodern plant equipped with giant presses capable of printing and binding 130,000 books a day. The Dreux Bindery, at one time a subsidiary of Firmin-Didot, also nearly shut down. Saved by a turnaround specialist, it today continues a long tradition of quality bookbinding in Dreux. Shoe manufacturing, which employed many locals at the turn of the century, had dwindled by the end of World War II to one small plant—Dreux's last link, as we shall see, to a settlement of freed convicts. That plant quietly closed its doors in the early 1960s.

The local foundry was still operating in 1945, but it was on its last legs. The largest plants in the city at that time were those of Grosdemouge, Facel, and Potez, firms specializing in metalworking and mechanical assembly and subcontractors to the aviation and automobile industries: the superb Facel-Vega automobiles were assembled in Dreux. These plants were not yet in existence when Maurice Viollette was first elected mayor; all opened for business in the period between the wars. In the 1950s they employed 150–200 workers each—elite workers, skilled metal "craftsmen," as people said in those days. In 1950 all the industrial firms in Dreux were family-owned, managed in a paternalistic fashion, and deeply involved in local life. There was nothing anonymous about them: a machinist's wife was apt to run into Madame Grosdemouge or the wife of the owner of Esmery-Caron in the marketplace.

None of the local factories was able to withstand the shock of modernization that France experienced during the "Thirty Glorious Years," the shock of international competition and the need to rationalize production for efficient, large-scale output. Grosdemouge was the first to succumb. The plant shut down in 1958. Facel followed after a long agony in 1964, and Potez's turn came in 1970. Only two large plants survived this period: Nomel and Beaufour. Nomel, a metalworking firm, employed lower-skilled workers than other local firms in the same branch of industry.[14] Beaufour had only recently begun its operations. This multinational pharmaceutical firm grew out of the researches of a Dreux pharmacist with a shop on Place Rotrou, where he first prepared the betaine citrate that became the basis of the company's first product. Beaufour belongs more to the industrial culture of the "second Dreux" that grew up on the ruins of the first; it does not draw on the local industrial tradition.

Businesses die, others take their place. Immediately after World War II, Paris and its surrounding region were overcrowded and literally choking on industry. In the early 1950s government planners forced Paris-based firms to loosen their grip in the hope of revitalizing the "French desert." Using a combination of zoning restrictions in Paris and tax incentives in the provinces, the government required firms based in or near Paris to search out new sites for future development. The Eure-et-Loir was too close to the capital to benefit from tax abatements. Dreux nevertheless emphasized all its advantages in an effort to entice new industry: the city was just an hour west of Paris, it had a strong industrial tradition, its workers were less demanding than workers in larger cities, and the city was at the center of a labor pool that local officials portrayed as abundant. Particularly important at a time of full employment, many of Dreux's workers needed new jobs because the city's old industries were gone.

The opening of the Radiotechnique facilities symbolizes the birth of the new industrial Dreux. Radiotechnique is an old French company, founded in 1919 to build vacuum tubes for radios. In 1931 it became part of the Philips group. After the end of World War II the firm grew rapidly. Its plant in Suresnes in the western suburbs of Paris could no longer meet the rapidly growing demand for its product, and management decided to look for new sites west of the capital. When Dreux officials learned of these plans, they proposed their city as a site for a new factory. Mayor Viollette told Radiotechnique executives that they would find land at attractive prices, offered the city's help in improving roads, powerlines, and other facilities, and guaranteed a plentiful supply of labor. The site was chosen, and Radiotechnique's two Dreux facilities opened their gates in 1956: a television assembly plant and a second plant for the manufacture of electronic components and cathode-ray tubes created more than a thousand new jobs.

Radiotechnique was not alone. Other firms employing more than two hundred workers came to Dreux in 1954–1975: Actime and Verboom in the metalworking branch, Rosi, Floquet-Monople, and Renault in the automobile sector, and Norgan in pharmaceuticals. Another new business began in the nearby town of Skaï, whose name has become synonymous with a kind of imitation leather. Between 1950 and 1970 twenty-five firms opened plants in the city of Dreux alone. Six thousand new jobs were created.[15] The new firms shared a number of features in common that distinguished them from the firms that made up the traditional industrial fabric of Dreux: their corporate headquarters were located outside Dreux (and, in the case of the artificial-leather firm, outside France), and they were labor-intensive operations, in many cases assembly plants employing unskilled workers.

Hiring Hands

The new companies were welcomed by local authorities as benefactors of the city. They created jobs and brought wealth to Dreux. Unfortunately, the displaced workers from Grosdemouge, Potez, the foundry, and, later, Firmin-Didot could not find work in the new firms: they were too skilled, demanded too much in wages, and were possibly too attached to unions whose influence the new managements feared. Modern assembly lines require docile workers willing to endure difficult conditions. The large labor pool that the mayor had touted to Radiotechnique turned out to be incapable of supplying enough of the right kind of workers. In 1956, when the first Radiotechnique plant was ready to begin operations, several hundred additional workers had to be found. A scholar who has studied the Radiotechnique move into the area west of Paris tells how the firm attempted to cope with the disastrous situation: "An extraordinary recruitment campaign was launched

. . . to bring in workers from Brittany. The personnel department from the Dreux plant set up an office in Hennebont [in Brittany] to select and train workers laid off by the Forges there. When this failed to produce sufficient numbers of workers, the company brought in Italians, Hungarians from a camp at Domfront, and Spaniards. Nearly five hundred workers were hired in this way . . . This solved the problem, but only temporarily, because the new work force proved unstable. It did, however, allow the plant to begin operations."[16] In the years that followed, Radiotechnique was again forced to hire foreign workers: its recruiters traveled to Italy, Spain, and Morocco in search of semiskilled labor. In 1970 some 39 percent of the workers employed in the plant were foreign-born.

The Radiotechnique situation was by no means unique. Most of the labor-intensive industrial firms that located in Dreux experienced similar difficulties with recruitment, particularly since they were offering for the most part relatively unskilled jobs. Each one developed its own favorite source of new workers: Skaï turned to Africa, Nomel to Portugal, and Comasec (which manufactures protective rubber garments) to Turkey.

City officials, eager to keep industry moving into Dreux, tried to find solutions to the manpower problem. One possibility turned up in 1962, when France granted Algeria independence to end the war. Many people left Algeria for France. Some were colonists of European origin who, unwilling to remain under the new regime installed by the National Liberation Front, returned to metropolitan France. But other refugees were more like exiles than repatriated Frenchmen. These so-called *harkis* and *moghaznis* were men and women of Muslim origin who had worked for or otherwise assisted the French army and civilian bureaucracy. The new Algerian government considered such people to be collaborators with the colonial power and threatened them with death or prison. Those who were able to leave Algeria were granted French nationality, but despite their service to France they did not always find a warm welcome on French soil. Unlike the *pieds noirs,* the returning settlers of European origin, who in the first months at least received an outpouring of assistance, few municipalities in France easily accepted Muslims who had chosen to become Frenchmen. Many of them wound up in refugee camps. Officials in Dreux looked upon these displaced North Africans as a much-needed source of manpower. The city gave a plot of land to Son-acotra, a semipublic agency charged with building workers' housing. Some two hundred apartments were hastily built for the newly arrived *harkis,* who moved into the long, narrow buildings that went up on the city's outskirts in 1963. Their arrival attracted virtually no attention at the time, and no one made an effort to welcome them to Dreux or to find out anything about them. Their only contact with official France was through a military officer who had been the commander of some of these men in Algeria and who felt a duty to help them and their families.

If ever there was a ghetto in Dreux in the strict sense of the word, it was this colony of *harkis:* for more than a decade, a group of people who had suffered the ravages of the civil and anticolonial war in Algeria lived in virtual isolation, nursing their misfortune, their cultural difference, and their internal conflicts. The men worked in the factories, the children went to school, but otherwise these people had no contact with the world around them. The women never left the housing compound. Today, over thirty years later, many of them still speak little French. To the residents of central Dreux, the housing project in which the immigrants lived, Murger-Bardin (more commonly known as Harki City), was nothing but a name. No Drouais ever went there, and most of the newcomers kept to themselves. When a handful of North African veterans of the French army decided to put on their old uniforms, decorated with medals won at Monte Cassino or Dien Bien Phu or Algeria, and march in the Armistice Day or V-E Day parades in town, their presence caused discomfort. When they tried to attend the annual veterans' banquet along with their former comrades, there were occasional incidents. Most of the North African families sensed this hostility and concentrated on forgetting the nightmare that had divided their country and in some cases their own flesh and blood. They gave their children French first names in the hope that they would eventually assimilate and disappear into the melting pot. For themselves they recognized that although their identity cards said they were French citizens and although they had suffered grievously for the blue, white, and red, the people of Dreux regarded them as foreigners. Even worse, they confused them with their former enemies, with the masses of Algerian immigrants indiscriminately branded as former partisans of the National Liberation Front. To the oldtime residents of Dreux, these *harkis* were *bicots* and *crouilles*—derogatory terms for Arabs—even though most of them came from Kabylia and spoke only Berber, not Arabic. They were nevertheless destined to become not only Frenchmen but Drouais. For them there was no home to return to.

Ex-Convicts

In the local argot of Dreux, there is a word that has been applied to newcomers ever since the nineteenth century. Until a stranger was familiar enough to be called by name, people would refer to that person as *l'accouru* (one who has come running). The term carries a hint of contempt, wariness, and suspicion. It was applied indiscriminately to all newcomers, to all for whom Dreux was not "home." A person did not have to come from a foreign country to be considered a foreigner. In other words, the border that separated Dreux and its surroundings from the rest of the world had nothing to do with any official boundary. In the past, Frenchmen measured distance in terms of time, and any place that one did not know was foreign.[17] Anyone whose history and ancestors one did not know was considered a foreigner. At the turn of the century, for instance, Maurice Viollette himself was an *accouru* when he first came to Dreux to run for the position of deputy. Though a native of the Eure-et-Loir, he hailed from a place far enough away to inspire distrust and fear: he was the son of a prominent citizen of Janville, a cantonal capital typical of the Beauce region and at the time more than a day's journey away from Dreux. This was another country.

In fact, one particular type of stranger, a common sight in Dreux before World War I, left an indelible mark on the town's collective memory. Under French law, former convicts, after being released from prison or a penal colony, could be forbidden to return to the places where they had committed their crimes; after settling elsewhere, they remained under surveillance for life. Discipline and punish, punish and discipline some more: Michel Foucault has analyzed the mechanisms of social control that developed around the nineteenth-century prison system. His work can help us to understand Dreux and its fears. Throughout the nineteenth century, Dreux was a link in this disciplinary chain. Free men and women turned out to gawk at notorious convicts being transported from Paris to Brest: "Most of the people in the crowd gathered outside the inn are from Créteil," *La Gazette des tribunaux* reported on 23 October 1829. "They come to catch a glimpse of Valentin, formerly a miller in that town. The sight of him is a feast for the eyes. Children point their fingers at him . . . They shout, 'It's Valentin, it's Valentin!' And he answers, 'Yes, it's Valentin, and if you don't behave, you'll end up where I am . . . And that's no joke. Let me be an example to you.' "[18] The newspaper report was intended to be edifying, for one purpose of transporting prisoners in chains was to reassure the law-abiding citizens and strike fear into the hearts of the wicked.

At some point in the 1960s a restaurant opened in Dreux under the name Vidocq. Someone remembered that in 1838 a gang of prisoners had stayed somewhere in the very street where the restaurant was located, perhaps in the same building. The whole town had turned out to witness a rare spectacle, because the famous criminal François-Eugène Vidocq (who survived imprisonment to become head of the Sûreté, or national police) was part of this gang. The fund of local memories was filled with images of prisoners who had spent a night in Dreux and whom people had turned out in large numbers to spit on or feel pity for. People were of course afraid that a prisoner might take advantage of the stop to break his chains and escape. The specter of a convict on the loose haunted the city.

Many prisoners who had served their time flocked to Dreux (and other towns on the fringes of the Paris basin). Having endured the wrath of the state, these men sought a quiet life after returning from a penal colony or prison. Dreux was as close to the capital as they were permitted to reside, and there were jobs to be had, so they came and stayed.

Although these ex-convicts were subject to regular surveillance, which made them, in effect, prisoners without walls for life and limited their movements, some were tempted to return to their old ways, broke the ban, and returned to Paris. Others settled in Dreux. Paul Prestat, for example, served five years in prison for robbery. After being released in 1850, he found a job with a man named Wolf, who ran a modest shoemaking business in Dreux. Thanks to his skill and initiative, Prestat soon formed a partnership with his erstwhile employer and developed the business into an important local industry. A letter that he sent to the mayor of Dreux in 1860, ten years after his arrival, attests to his business success as well as to the constraints imposed on him as an ex-convict: "Good fortune has made me a partner in a firm employing eighty men and women. We have business relations with at least five hundred clients . . . The needs of the business require me to take short trips within a radius of twenty leagues. It is impossible for me to take such trips, however, because I am under surveillance as an ex-convict . . . I am writing to obtain not exoneration for my crimes but permission, at least, to travel without being arrested as a vagabond for violation of the ban. Since M. Wolf, who can barely read or write, is incapable of running the business, such a misfortune, if it were to arrive, would impose an intolerable burden on our business."[19]

Prestat's case was unusual, to be sure. The several hundred ex-convicts who became residents of Dreux in the nineteenth century rarely enjoyed such spectacular success. Most lived on the fringes of local society in furnished rooms in the less reputable parts of town. They drank in the same bars and taverns. And their reputation was poor. Throughout the century, mayor after mayor beseeched the prefect of the département not to send any more ex-convicts to Dreux. There were too many of them (including a few women), and besides being dubious, potentially dangerous individuals, they were apt to take work from law-abiding citizens.

Memories of Dreux's role as a dumping ground for ex-convicts linger on, even though the practice has long since been eliminated. Some have argued in recent years that the reason why Dreux has had to take in so many *accourus,* so many outsiders, is that the government has always regarded it as an open city, a place to send ex-convicts unwelcome anywhere else. It does no good to point out that the French penal system is no longer what it was: many residents of Dreux continue to believe that their city was chosen by Paris to receive the dregs of the earth. What other explanation could there possibly be, they ask, for the presence of so many new faces? This myth continues to flourish at all levels of local society, even among the most recently arrived. As late as February 1990 I heard an Algerian-born industrial instructor tell his students that there were foreigners in Dreux because Dreux is an open city.

Saturday Nights

Before winning acceptance and recognition, newcomers, even if not just out of prison, were expected to prove that they could fit in. Just after World War II there were groups and organizations that helped new arrivals find their place in local society. People who have lived through the experience say it was not easy. In those days, however, political parties, trade unions, churches, and neighborhood groups still served as mediators between the newcomer and the city, facilitating integration.

The peripheral neighborhoods closest to the center of town were still villages. Places like Saint-Thibault, Le Bois-Sabot, and

Les Rochelles were known as *communes libres*. In other words, they were as Montmartre is to Paris: administratively part of Dreux but with a distinctive identity of their own. Dreux's *communes libres* had mayors of their own, whose principal function was to make plans for an annual neighborhood festival. The people of the neighborhood contributed to this event, which demonstrated the area's distinctive character. Newcomers who were not antisocial could participate in the preparations and gradually make friends. Anyone willing to sell tickets, set up a merry-go-round, or play the accordion was welcome.

Until the 1960s it was relatively easy for immigrants to find local clubs or organizations that suited their interests. The man who was not a veteran could join a hunting or fishing club or work with the PTA or root for the local soccer team. All these groups brought people together and staged annual dances. Not a Saturday went by without a dance organized by some local group. These events took place in the dance hall in the center of town. Some, like those organized by the Union Commerciale or La Marine, were stylish, expensive affairs with music provided by a Parisian orchestra. Others were aimed at people of more modest means, with entertainment provided by a local band. Take, for example, the annual dance staged by the apprentices in training at the local watchmakers' school. The school's graduates were nationally renowned for their skills, and its annual dance had a certain panache: it opened with a lancers' quadrille. During the week before the dance, the young apprentices went in their navy-blue uniforms to ask the fathers of the town's young women for permission to escort their daughters to the dance. Merchants were especially fond of these young men, who would soon begin working in a time-honored craft. They would make quite suitable sons-in-law. Thus invitations to the dance were greeted with a certain solemnity: who knew what might come of one?

Dances, no matter which group organized them, were a place for people to meet, though social differences persisted. Sometimes those differences were evident in the physical appearance of the dance hall: wealthier guests tended to reserve tables (those closest to the orchestra were the most highly prized), whereas working people when not dancing were apt to remain standing at the back of the hall. Refreshments were available in the lobby. Yet people danced together despite their differences, which the festive night-time atmosphere tended to diminish. A dancer's skill mattered more than social status. Local politicians made their obligatory appearance around midnight as guests of the group staging the dance. If the mayor and other local officials failed to show up, that group might easily feel slighted, and the consequences of such an affront could prove serious at the next election. Politicians who came were rewarded for their diligence: after shaking hands they might make a couple of rounds of the dance floor before returning home, satisfied at having "pressed the flesh" of a substantial number of voters.

The tradition of weekend dances and neighborhood parties peaked in the 1950s. Block parties began going out of fashion in the 1960s and weekend dances in the following decade. Styles of working and living were changing in Dreux, and the city's population was growing. The old forms of socializing disappeared, and no new ones emerged to take their place, even as the population was absorbing large numbers of newcomers.

The Population Doubles (1954–1975)

Postwar industrialization led to marked changes in Dreux's demographic characteristics. These changes constitute a sharp break in the city's history, even though one cannot date the break precisely, as if it were a single event. It was not so much an immediately perceptible fact as a process, a series of phenomena all but unnoticed as they occurred. The magnitude of the change becomes evident only when we examine the statistical charts, plot the numbers in graphs, and examine the data in the context of what historians call "extended time." When we do all this, we see that Dreux's demographic evolution from 1954 to 1975 amounted to nothing less than a revolution—a quiet revolution, to be sure, yet more fraught with consequences for the city's future than all the wars it was forced to endure.

In 1900 Dreux's population was 9,718. Over the previous century its population had increased but not quite doubled. After World War I, the population continued to increase despite the war's casualties and the consequent shortage of young men and the low birth rate. Families that had given up farming settled in Dreux, as did Italians fleeing fascism and, in 1939, Spanish republicans fleeing Franco. When World War II ended, the population stood at slightly more than 14,000: Dreux was a large town.

The city as we know it today was born in the mid-1950s. The growth rate accelerated suddenly. Within twenty years the population doubled, from 16,818 in 1954 to 33,095 in 1975. In this respect Dreux was by no means unique. Cities throughout France increased in population by slightly more than 15 million over the same period. This urban growth was proof that France, which stayed rural much later than most other developed countries, had regained its vitality. The country was simply making up for lost time. So what was there to worry about?

People in Dreux were delighted to hear at each new census that the population of their city had reached record heights. Not only was the population increasing, but most of the new people were young and full of energy. To city officials, the influx of new residents was evidence of success. Dreux seemed blessed by nature, moreover: though close to the capital, it retained its provincial charm; located at the confluence of three river valleys, its setting was beautiful; and it was the right size, for this was a time when medium-sized cities were in vogue. Dreux was in many ways typical of the time, the very embodiment of the phrase "quality of life" as it was in the late 1960s and early 1970s, when there was a great deal of enthusiasm for living in cities small enough to promise newcomers easy integration into urban life. Big cities were frightening, but smaller ones were considered more human in scale. Mayors of medium-sized cities fought to maintain a "reasonable" population. The mayor of Saumur, for example, was willing to allow his city to develop economically as long as it "remained on a human scale." The mayor of Colmar, meanwhile, expressed a "wish to avoid urbanization on a gigantic scale." Tarbes, according to its mayor, was modern "but not gigantic to the point of inevitably dampening human warmth and creating problems. We want to remain a middle-sized city, to preserve our human character."[20]

The mayor of Dreux, Jean Cauchon, boasted of his city's growth and never gave a speech without reminding his audience that "Dreux is a city where the living is good." Dreux, in other words, was one of a number of modest cities about which there was little to say other than that they had felt the winds of modernization. Already, however, the growing population was beginning to create today's problems: rundown working-class housing, insecurity, social tension, and political instability.

From 1801 to 1900 Dreux gained an average of fifty new residents each year through natural increase plus immigration. From 1900 to 1950 the average annual increase rose to eighty-eight. But from 1954 to 1968 it rose to a thousand. Between 1962 and 1968 it reached 1,220. The city could no longer be contained within its old boundaries. Up to the Liberation, Dreux was surrounded by small villages. These now grew at a very rapid pace, more rapidly than the city itself, and their character along with their population changed from agricultural to industrial. A veritable urban center (city and suburbs) came into being. Between 1962 and 1968 the population of this center increased by an average of more than 1,600 persons annually.

In cities like Paris, Marseilles, or Lyons an extra 1,600 people would mean little or nothing. In Dreux it meant that each year the population increased by roughly 10 percent, with the newcomers being drawn from outside the area. When the number of new residents each year amounted to no more than a few dozen, the new arrivals were noticed, to be sure, and perhaps even looked at with suspicion, but in the end they became familiar, recognized members of the community. Still, the addition of more than a thousand new faces every year was bewildering. Before long, older residents had the sense that they were no longer completely at home in their own birthplace.

But population statistics alone are insufficient to explain the astonishing changes that occurred in Dreux in those years of prosperity. The doubling of the population took place in chaotic conditions, which saw many working men and whole families arrive only to depart again and be replaced by others. For many immigrants from Normandy and Brittany, Yugoslavia and Tunisia, Dreux was only a stopping place en route to somewhere else.

The mobility of the new working population is reflected in studies of Radiotechnique employees in the 1950s: "Plant managers are generally silent on the subject of employment problems, but the figures on job turnover show clearly that problems did exist. While the number of departures in all plants did decrease over time and employees tended to remain on the job longer as plant conditions became more stable, it is nevertheless true that job turnover was extremely rapid . . . For example, over the three-year period from 1958 to 1960, more than 70 percent of the hourly personnel left their jobs in the Chartres plant. In Chartres and Dreux the entire workforce has had to be replaced."[21]

Newcomers Named Mohammed

Until the late 1960s former peasants from Normandy and Brittany far outnumbered foreign immigrants among the newcomers to Dreux, though it is impossible to give precise figures. These French immigrants, uprooted from their native soil, not only met with a cool reception from Dreux natives but also had to accustom themselves to hard industrial labor. Yet they overcame these hurdles more rapidly when a sort of tacit common front developed in the 1970s, uniting newcomers of French and European origin against immigrants from North Africa and Turkey.

I seriously and permanently offended the Bretons of Dreux

when I stated in a 1982 television broadcast that the North Africans in the city were, all things considered, victims of prejudices comparable to those that the Bretons themselves had faced when they settled in Dreux in the 1950s and 1960s. Didn't Dreux old-timers in those days insist that the city was most generous to provide gleaming new apartment buildings for peasants who had known only shacks in their native Brittany? Didn't those peasants store coal in their bathtubs and slaughter chickens in the lobbies of their apartment houses? By 1982 the Bretons were "integrated." They didn't like being compared to Arabs who slaughtered sheep in their bathrooms (so it was said), though a few women were moved during one local radio broadcast to admit that the comparison was not without foundation. Some of those Breton women even compared the hostility aroused when they wore the traditional Bigouden headdress to mass twenty years earlier to the violent attacks on Muslim women for wearing veils.

Population figures at any given moment are mere aggregates, bloodless averages, that hide the faces of individuals and their complex destinies. They do, however, shed light on the sheer magnitude of the changes affecting Dreux and thus begin to tell the story of how an old order gave way to what would soon be perceived as disorder.

The new immigrants who began to arrive from the southern shores of the Mediterranean in the late 1950s were not seen in the same way as previous newcomers. They showed no signs of becoming permanent residents of Dreux, so that locals thought of them as people in transit, as a necessary but temporary evil. In any case they were not much in evidence. They kept to themselves, living in dormitories or in furnished rooms hastily made ready by the owners of older apartment buildings. During the 1960s one rarely saw immigrant workers in Dreux except at the post office, where long lines formed at the end of every month—this was the first source of irritation with the "foreigners," who were sending their wages home to their families. Often it took a long time for them to transact their business, not least because the postal employees behind the counter could not always understand what they were saying. Critics chastised them for contributing nothing to the city, since they lived on very little, spending no more than was strictly necessary. Basically, though, the money orders sent home to Algeria or Portugal were viewed as a reassuring sign that these immigrants planned one day to leave. This conviction was reinforced by the fact that many of them actually did return home. But they were immediately replaced by others, for whom the future seemed to hold much the same fate. How many foreigners passed through Dreux between 1954 1975? One thing is certain: the number who passed through far exceeded the number who remained. People in Dreux thus naturally believed that all the foreigners who came to their city would one day return home.

It was not until 1971 that municipal officials first began to show signs of anxiety about the influx of immigrants. In the spring of that year a near-tragic event brought quiet little Dreux notice in the national press for something other than an aristocratic wedding in the royal chapel—namely, immigration. A Redemptorist seminary in the heart of town that had closed down for lack of novices had been transformed into a reception center for new immigrant workers, mostly from Africa and the Maghreb. One night a fire raced through the building. Was it an accident? Investigators blamed a camp stove that had not been fully extinguished. But rumors of a racist attack also circulated. In July 1971 a journalist from *Le Monde* came to Dreux to investigate. He reported that Mayor Cauchon felt that "the foreign population had reached the danger level" and had asked the prefect "to take steps to stop the influx of foreign nationals." Citizens of Dreux complained of being afraid to go out at night lest they encounter one of the many lonely foreign men who roamed the city's streets. The reporter also quoted a Dreux employer who preferred to remain anonymous: "Either the government will have to provide facilities for dealing with the new arrivals, or my factory will have to slow production for lack of manpower and possibly 'emigrate' at some point in the future."[22]

At the beginning of 1970 there were 3,622 foreigners in Dreux, or 11 percent of the population. Had the mayor sensed that pressures were increasing? By the end of 1971 there were 4,211 foreigners, an increase of 16 percent in one year. Had the mayor realized that, despite the good will displayed on the night of the fire (all the foreigners found temporary lodging with "natives"), xenophobic sentiment was on the rise? In any case he tried to shift responsibility for the immigrants to the national government. The companies that built plants in industrial parks developed by the city were openly recruiting workers abroad. The "immigration question" was now raised publicly for the first time. Jean Rambaud, the *Le Monde* reporter, ended his article with these words: "In the intervals between incidents and crises, it may be that the only option for Dreux—and for all of us—is to strike some kind of balance."

Striking a balance. In a time of prosperity this was already difficult to do, yet not out of reach. When hard times struck, however, the possibility of maintaining a delicate equilibrium all but evaporated.

Crucible and Crisis

· 2 ·

Yesterday in Dreux explains today, provided one understands the extent to which twenty-five years of unprecedented growth turned the city upside-down and fifteen years of deep recession left it battered and bruised. The turmoil proved bitter for individuals as well as for the city, all the more so because it afflicted an organism that was fragile to begin with. City officials, in their euphoria over the kind of economic development that the region endured without prior planning, did not foresee the consequences of urbanization, the failure to create service-sector jobs, and an increased dependence on outside capital (and decisionmakers). Nor did they worry about living conditions in the housing projects that proliferated on the heights. As far back as 1971, Mayor Jean Cauchon foresaw the danger of xenophobia triggered by a growing foreign population. At the time, antiforeign sentiment was more a vague attitude than an ingrained opinion. Yet Cauchon was among the first to blame foreign immigration for the profound urban crisis.

Foreign workers were merely the symptom of a condition whose causes have yet to be fully analyzed. It was easy to blame foreigners whose customs were strange and to suggest that, if only the government wished, immigration could be halted tomorrow and all the foreigners sent home the next day; such notions raised the false hope that Dreux could somehow regain the small-town atmosphere it once had. Although it was simplistic to blame all of the city's problems on its foreign population, this explanation caught on and has wide currency today. True, by the 1980s Jean Cauchon and other early critics of immigration had become vocal opponents of the xenophobes. But by the mid-1970s the elements of Dreux's present-day climate were already in place. Combined, they formed an explosive mixture that needed only a spark to set it off.

The End of Growth

When economic and demographic growth declined, there were major social and political consequences for Dreux. Between 1950 and 1970 the city bore the brunt of a demographic explosion for which it was totally unprepared. It met the emergency by building large numbers of new housing units. With each new schoolyear it became necessary to set up prefabricated classrooms to accommodate students not anticipated in the previous year's planning. In the early 1970s Dreux officials attempted to predict the consequences of further development. One 1975 forecast envisioned that by 1990 Dreux would be the center of an urbanized region of 80,000 people. City-hall bureaucrats set about planning for the future on the basis of this forecast. These delusions of grandeur on the part of local officials were confirmed by the confident predictions of bureaucrats at the national level that steady economic growth would continue. On the heights west of the city, in an area that had until then maintained an agricultural character, ground was broken for a new housing complex, a veritable city within a city planned to accommodate an unbelievable 20,000 new citizens.

At the national level economists set the tone. In 1973 Jean-Jacques Carré, Paul Dubois, and Edmond Malinvaud published the *Abrégé de la croissance française* (A Primer on French Growth), which immediately became the bible of students of economics. The word "unemployment" is virtually absent from the text. Prospects for the future were glowing or, at any rate, would be glowing if the French economy were not threatened by "exhaustion of the reserves of manpower underemployed or poorly employed in agriculture." The authors concluded that "all things considered, the extraordinary development that France, along with many other countries, has experienced since the war seems . . . unlikely to slow substantially in the foreseeable future. Rising levels of output and standards of living will surely constitute the most important economic phenomenon of the second half of the twentieth century."[1] What reason was there for people living in a small French city that had shared in the "extraordinary development" of the postwar years to think otherwise?

Yet the Dreux economy, without showing any clear signs of a slowdown, had already, along with the French economy as a whole, entered a new phase, even before the oil shock triggered by the 1973 OPEC embargo set off a round of instability that reverberated throughout the economies of the free world. With hindsight, signs of a downturn can be perceived in Dreux as early as the mid-1960s, and economic historians have noted the same indications at the national level. After 1965, for example, there were fewer factory openings in Dreux compared with those a generation ago, and these openings created fewer new jobs. Had the economy merely slowed, or had things really turned around? It is only in retrospect that the magnitude of the recession becomes apparent. At the time, people felt that the head of steam built up over past decades would carry them through. But the rate of population growth had declined. Even as new housing projects were going up and new neighborhoods were being planned, Dreux, unbeknownst to its leaders, had ceased to be an industrially attractive city. Fewer outside workers were coming in. Between 1968 and 1975 the population increased by only 3,000, or an annual growth rate of 1.7 percent compared with 5.3 percent from 1962 to 1968. What is more, the influx of people from outside the area, which had accounted for most of the population growth since the war, ceased to be the most important demographic factor. In fact, between 1968 and 1975 the city of Dreux itself experienced a net outflow of population, even as the surrounding region continued to draw newcomers in considerable numbers. To be sure, some of those who left Dreux moved into the surrounding communities. Yet the birth rate now became the major factor contributing to population growth, and since the birth rate remains high, the city continues to grow. Indeed, most of the immigration of the previous two decades involved young couples, who had children. In 1975 one out of five residents of Dreux was under ten years of age, and four out of ten attended school. With a birth rate of 27.2 per 1,000 (compared with 17 per 1,000 nationwide), Dreux is an unusually young and fertile city. Whereas only 14.5 percent of the French population as a whole is under the age of ten, 20 percent of the population of Dreux is; yet only 10.9 percent of Drouais are over sixty, compared with 18.9 percent of the French generally.

Between 1968 and 1975 the number of jobs available decreased very slowly. The decrease was scarcely noticed because unemployment was still rare. The Agence Nationale pour l'Emploi (National Employment Bureau, or ANPE) did not yet exist. The local employment office was housed in a wooden shack that dated back to the German occupation. Every morning the same people showed up: a few derelicts who hoped to find work for a day or two sweeping floors or sidewalks (and sometimes they got lucky). The adjustment of the supply of jobs to demand did not take place in this rickety bureaucratic outpost, however. The job market was still self-regulating and no administrative intervention was required, except on the margins. The big employers in the area still recruited their own workers from abroad and provided transportation to Dreux without even availing themselves of the services of the National Immigration Office, except when necessary to convert tourist visas to working visas, which could be done on the spot. This practice was not peculiar to Dreux: between 1960 and 1970, nearly 65 percent of foreign workers resolved difficulties with their working papers right on the job site.

Nor did the local middle class turn to the employment office for domestic help. In the 1950s, housewives drove twenty or thirty miles out into the Perche, a region where, until the turn of the century, rural women had earned extra money by serving as wet nurses to infants from Parisian families and who now looked to city folk to hire them as maids. Every self-respecting household in Dreux had contacts in some rural village. But young rural women willing to do domestic work became increasingly rare and they demanded higher wages: factories competed with households for their services. So young women from abroad filled the need. The fashionable housewife of the 1960s had a Portuguese or Spanish maid, most likely a woman who came to join her mason or factory-hand husband and who dreamed of one day returning home and building her own house with what she and her husband managed to save during their time in France. These women were highly prized: not only were they good workers but, even more important, they did not want their income declared.

Unemployed Workers and Proletarians

By 1970 the economy was stagnant but had not yet gone into a recession. It was not until 1974 that the number of individuals seeking work surpassed the number of jobs available. Although some very small businesses were still creating new jobs, many firms began laying off workers, reducing working hours, and cutting their work force. The tight job market was due in part to short-term problems in the economy, in part to modernization of the production process. In 1976 the real crisis hit, and the number of unemployed grew dramatically. Two large companies began cutting their work force. Skaï, which had employed 500 workers in 1973, reduced that number by half, and Actime shut its plant, throwing nearly 500 workers and supervisory personnel out of work. All told, some 1,000 jobs disappeared in late 1976 and early 1977. The impact was severe. Until then, all that people in Dreux knew about the recession was what they learned from the national newspapers and television. Locals felt that they had been spared, never suspecting that huge factories sporting the signs of internationally known firms might be vulnerable to hard times. Now they began to see factory after factory boarded up and offered for sale, and month after month, year after year, no buyers appeared. Radiotechnique, the symbol of Dreux's entry into the modern economic era, began laying off workers in 1979. In that same year Skaï closed its vast operations for good, and for a long time its plants in the Dreux area remained an industrial wasteland. Next, in 1982, came the turn of Firmin-Didot: all its employees were let go.

In less than ten years, from 1975 to 1985, the city and its surrounding area experienced an abrupt reversal of fortune. What happened in Dreux, of course, was far less dramatic than what was happening at the same time in northern and eastern France, where the collapse of the textile and steel industries and the closing of iron and coal mines disrupted life across vast sections of the country. Events in Dreux were also dwarfed by the consequences of the closing of naval shipyards all along the coast from Dunkirk to La Ciotat, including Nantes and Saint-Nazaire. Dreux, though, was a disaster area by anybody's standards: "Between December 1974 and December 1977, the number of job applicants unable to find work doubled. In 1977 the Dreux region was the third hardest-hit in central France. By early 1980, nearly 7 percent of the working population was unemployed in the Dreux zone of the ANPE, where there were three applicants for every job. By late October 1983 the unemployment rate had risen to 10 percent, giving Dreux a most unwelcome record high for the département."[2]

The recession revealed just how proletarian the city had become during its growth period. Changes in the occupational structure of the population reveal this quite clearly. In the period 1954–1975, the number of blue-collar workers increased by a factor of 3.2. The number of skilled workers doubled, while the number of semiskilled workers quintupled. Whereas skilled workers made up 58.3 of the working population in 1954, their proportion had shrunk to just 35 percent in 1975 (the other 65 percent being semiskilled). As the city developed, the skill level of its population declined.

During the recession, moreover, it was the least skilled workers who were thrown out of work and into long-term unemployment—a kind of unemployment from which it is very difficult if not impossible to escape.

Large firms were the first to feel the effects of the recession. Hundreds of families experienced the shock of unemployment at the same time. The first plant closings triggered a chain reaction: small subcontractors and service firms that had been in business with the big companies were forced to cut back or, in some cases, to shut down. In industry the least skilled jobs were the first to go. Dreux's growth had been due in large part to labor-intensive industries: the new plants used relatively cheap manpower rather than costly machines. Moreover, the construction industry, which used large numbers of laborers, collapsed once the population stopped growing.

Many of the people who lost their jobs in Dreux lost them permanently. It turned out that men who had worked ten, fifteen, or twenty years for one company did not know how to read, write, or do arithmetic: these handicaps had not hindered them in their jobs, so no one had bothered with remedial training. Now they were stigmatized as illiterate. Just to apply for a job or even for one of the retraining programs sponsored by the ANPE, they were expected to be able to read and write. A survey conducted in one Dreux neighborhood in 1989 revealed that "more than a third of the adult population over the age of eighteen can neither read nor write." This figure was merely an estimate, moreover, for it was "based on self-descriptions . . . unsubstantiated by any testing . . . and may therefore be regarded as a minimum."[3] To be sure, the residents of the part of town in which the survey was conducted were foreigners, but not all of them were newcomers. Take Habib, for example: "At age eighteen, when he embarked on the ship that would take him to France, he did not know how to read or write and could barely speak the [French] language. While working in the foundries of Moselle, in the construction industry, and for Radiotechnique in Dreux, where he was hired in 1973, he hardly needed those abilities."[4] Habib, who is over fifty today, grew up in French Algeria. He has lived and worked in France for thirty-two years. For the past seventeen years, he has been a resident of Dreux. His children were born in the city and attended the neighborhood school. Is he to blame for the fact that he can neither read nor write?

It should be noted too that illiteracy is not a problem limited to those of foreign birth or foreign ancestry. Government sources estimate that there are more than five million people in France who meet the UNESCO criterion for illiteracy: "Inability to read and understand a simple text pertaining to everyday life." The inescapable fact is that it was not necessary to read or write in order to work on an assembly line at Skaï or on a public construction project. Workers who once filled such jobs are now being asked to fill out forms, do calculations, and write reports and they are simply unable to perform those tasks.

Dreux's growth period (1954–1968) created a demographic situation that compounded the problem of proletarianization: by the mid-1970s the children of the workers who had flocked to Dreux during the expansionist phase were beginning to enter the labor market. Most of them were unskilled, but they were looking for work at a time when modernized industries were hiring skilled workers capable of running sophisticated new machines. Many of these young people left school at age sixteen. Sometimes their parents fought to have them admitted to an occupational training program, but openings were scarce and the selection criteria strict. Lacking credentials and skills, these young workers filed applications with the ANPE or one of its affiliates: often they were enrolled in some temporary job program, but these were dead ends for all but the most resourceful youths who, after moving from one temporary job to another for several years, managed to find medium-term or even long-term employment. Twenty years earlier, local firms justified their recruitment of foreign workers on the grounds that French workers were unwilling to do hard work for low wages. The very workers who had not turned up their noses at these arduous and sometimes dangerous jobs now constituted the majority of those who lined up in front of the ANPE's local office. Meanwhile, employers complained that they couldn't find the skilled workers they were looking for. In the period 1980–1985, for example, the demand for skilled workers so far outran the supply that some local firms were forced to recruit machinists from Lorraine.

The Old Town and the Rest

The demographic and industrial changes that took place during the years of prosperity radically and rapidly transfromed the urban landscape. As always in speaking of Dreux, one must distinguish between the old town, which remained virtually unchanged, and the surrounding heights. New housing sprang up mainly on the hills above the town. Between 1954 and 1975 the number of housing units more than doubled as new buildings were erected hastily and with no overall plan (the first city plan was not completed until 1968). Large apartment complexes—on a scale that overwhelmed existing buildings—were preferred to individual homes for no better reason than the urgency of the need for housing. Low-rent public projects predominated over housing built with private funds. In the second half of the 1950s, apartment buildings grew like mushrooms.

As the housing industry went, so went Dreux. The new projects, built by Portuguese masons on streets paved by Moroccan and Turkish laborers, were mere names to the people of central Dreux. The same names that had once designated wheat fields now identified housing projects: Le Murger, Les Bergeronnettes, Le Lièvre d'Or, La Croix Tiennac, La Mare Gallot—picturesque names redolent of rural life. Situated on heights where they could not be seen from the Grande Rue, the new districts formed a world apart. No one can understand the first thing about Dreux without appreciating the gulf that separated the old town from the rest. In other towns people speak of the center and the periphery, but in

Dreux it is "the city" and "the heights." As seen from central Dreux, the heights are unknown territory. And as seen from the heights, central Dreux represents a history in which the newcomers had no part. Such is the town's geography.

It may seem strange that topography has assumed such importance in this small place. As one who was born in the center of town, who spent a childhood in the suburbs, and who lived for a time in a working-class neighborhood on the heights before returning to the city, I can attest that one's view or conception of Dreux depends on where one lives. As the sociologist Pierre Bourdieu has said, "It is through spatial structures that mental structures take shape."[5] What is true of Paris is also true of Dreux: in this respect the size of a city makes no difference. A wall or a boulevard or even an ordinary street can form a barrier so impermeable that different cultures subsist on either side. People from one side of the line know nothing about people on the other side. During my tenure as mayor I visited schools on the heights where I met children who went "down into town" only twice a year, for the Saint-Denis Fair and the Bastille Day fireworks. Merchants with stores on the Grande Rue told me that they had never heard of the Les Bergeronnettes housing project, less than two miles away as the crow flies. Others said that they knew about the Chamards project only because they had noticed its towers in the distance when driving home from Paris.

The center of Dreux lies at the bottom of a valley. The posh streets and chic buildings—posh and chic by Dreux standards at least—are reassuring, as bourgeois comforts sometimes are. Here wealthy and fashionable people eyed one another jealously but made common cause against the invaders. One of the battlegrounds in the clash between the old city and the new was the Godeau School. Every attempt to revise the district boundaries of the school set off alarm bells among parents, who organized to defend the "standards" of an institution that was among the first public schools established under the Third Republic. Setting political differences aside, right and left joined forces around this issue. Both were willing to do whatever was necessary to prevent students in outlying housing projects from attending Godeau. According to the map, those projects should have fallen within the Godeau district, but they were inhabited by Turks, and therefore it was only natural that they should send their children to the "school for foreigners" on the southern heights where there were already so many other Turkish youngsters. Until his retirement in 1990, moreover, the principal of Godeau, an orthodox communist much admired by the local bourgeoisie for his traditional educational philosophy and his strict Third Republic style of discipline, was for a long time an outspoken opponent of city hall on this issue, for periodically the mayor attempted to include the project within the Godeau district. Whenever an attempt was made, the principal discreetly arranged to enroll French students who normally would not have been allowed to attend Godeau. With these additional students on the rolls, it was possible to argue that the Turkish youngsters could not be accommodated.

When I was mayor, my own nieces became beneficiaries of the principal's willingness to bend the rules. Because of where they lived, the girls should have attended the school on the northern heights, not Godeau. But the principal agreed to let them in. Godeau was proud of educating the children of the local elite, whose members needed no *Who's Who?* to know who belonged and who did not. In this and other ways the people of central Dreux protected themselves. They felt beleaguered because the population of the heights, beyond the older developments of single-family homes, consisted essentially of newcomers who were also foreign-born and working-class. They were, in a word, *barbarians,* separated from the old city by a boundary line that existed not on any map but in people's minds. People who regarded themselves as the descendants of the Gauls behaved as the Romans had behaved toward foreigners in the era just after the birth of Christ.

Two new districts that sprang up during the postwar prosperity symbolized the new city, each in its own way. One, known as

Prod'homme, stands on the far side of National Highway 12, which divides the northern heights into two parts, one regarded as decent by the people of the central city, the other as beyond the pale. The other, Les Chamards, stands on the southern heights, cut off from the center by a railway line.

Prod'homme: Excluded Frenchmen

The Prod'homme district is the oldest of the new sections.[6] In 1950 the area, which sits on the border between Dreux and an adjacent hamlet, was barren but for a few wooden barracks built in the 1940s to house refugees. In 1951, as newcomers flocked to the city and were unable to find housing, thirty so-called low-rent units were built to accommodate them: these were small, minimally equipped cabins that the people of central Dreux immediately took to calling "rabbit hutches." When seen at a distance from a car speeding past on the highway, these shacks do in fact look more like farm outbuildings than houses.

The new units were assigned to families that were very poor or had been judged incapable of adapting to life in a modern city and were therefore turned away from other public housing. In 1954 these exiles looked on as surveyors went to work in their neighborhood: fifty more units, now referred to as starter homes, went up at this time. The construction was even more rudimentary, for the new huts had slant rather than pent roofs. The money saved made it possible to charge rents low enough to attract families classified as "antisocial." In 1956 an additional hundred units were built, one right on top of the next. These were called "municipal refuge units." According to the minutes of one city council meeting, their purpose was to "house expelled or antisocial tenants and others of similar type." This expansion soon proved insufficient. In 1961 another ninety units were added under a national program known as "social rehousing." Public housing officials in charge called the project the Cité des Aubépines, or Hawthorn Housing—a lovely name. This was Dreux's solution to the problem of how to house "difficult populations": pack them together on the outskirts of town. Out of sight, out of mind: all but invisible, they bothered nobody.

Of course anyone who read the local papers knew that some strange things were going on in Prod'homme. There were gangs and gang battles, and guns and knives were part of everyday life. All over Dreux—in the central city and even in the single-family homes on the slopes—the mere mention of Prod'homme was enough to call up images of violence, drunkenness, drugs, and prostitution. Any youngster from Prod'homme was immediately classified as an actual or potential juvenile delinquent. And the crime columns of the local paper did indeed devote considerable space to adolescents and youths from the district. Their names alone—"real French names"—were enough to inspire fear. Many of these young people came from large families, and they were by no means affable, at least when first approached. When people from Prod'homme appeared in town, they were greeted with suspicion. If a resident of the district wished to pay for purchases by check, the merchant would carefully scrutinize her identification. Yet not one resident of Prod'homme was a foreigner, even if many were poor and all were in one way or another outcasts, casualties of modernization. Most were farmers who had left the land but had not been able to adapt to the rules of the urban industrial jungle.

The people who lived in Prod'homme basically loved the neighborhood, where conflict was merely a negative aspect of a genuine communal life. In 1962 Prod'homme's isolation from the rest of Dreux became more radical: the route of the Paris-Brest highway, which previously had passed through the center of town, was now changed so that it cut the northern heights in two. Prod'homme now lay outside the highway, on the side away from downtown Dreux, in an area where the city had already constructed a municipal landfill and would soon build a waste-treatment plant. The highway separating Prod'homme from downtown, meanwhile, handled 20,000 vehicles a day. Residents who needed to get to town, including children on their way to school, had to cross this heavily traveled route. Fatalities were inevitable. City officials did not even insist that highway engineers install a traffic light.

The population of Prod'homme has always been French. In 1963 a *harki* family from Algeria moved into the district. For many years, this was the only foreign family, and it was fully integrated into the neighborhood microsociety. Construction proceeded on adjacent vacant land to provide housing for additional "difficult cases" in the area beyond the highway. A high-rise housing project (Les Bergeronnettes) went up in 1968 not far from Hawthorn Housing and Prod'homme. The buildings in the project resemble candy bars. Once again, the nomenclature had changed: officially this was dubbed "reduced-rent housing." The project provided 180 low-rent apartments in an area exposed to the west wind, so that nothing could grow; once again the residents were outcasts, but now some of them were foreigners, including Portuguese and North Africans whose children would attend the Paul Bert School alongside French youngsters from Prod'homme.

Les Chamards: "All the World's Misery"

The second district I shall examine was developed on the heights south of Dreux in the early 1960s. To city officials at the time it symbolized the advent of a new era in Dreux. Today it stands as a symbol of faulty city planning in the years of prosperity, and sad pictures of what it has become have appeared in such publications as *Paris-Match, Le Nouvel Observateur, La Vie,* and *L'Evénement du jeudi.* The pictures show green spaces in which nothing green has grown for a long time, gutted mailboxes, smashed glass doors. French and foreign television crews in search of images to illustrate reports on the impoverished living conditions of immigrants in France or on the failure of immigration know that they can always find what they are looking for here.

The miserable conditions at Les Chamards suggest that this is a public housing project for the poor, but that is not the case. It is a private apartment complex built by a consortium of insurance companies and private developers. All told, there are some 830 apartments here, distributed among fifteen towers up to fifteen stories high. Until the middle of 1990 the buildings were managed by two different corporate entities with no ties to the community. Built on a wasteland on the southern fringes of Dreux, these impersonal towers remained for a long time cut off from the central city. At first the project was inhabited mainly by French families. But it proved too large for the needs of the city, which failed to grow as fast as predicted, and in the early 1970s it became a dormitory for automobile workers employed in the Seine valley, mostly North Africans. As these men lingered on in France, their hopes of returning home diminished, and many were joined by their families. Their employers, who needed their services and wanted to keep them on the job, found housing for them, and relatively recent arrivals were often steered toward Les Chamards. Dreux was a long way from the plants in which these men worked, but Renault, Chrysler, and Talbot provided transportation in company buses, which ran day and night. This was only a temporary solution, however, until apartments were ready in one of the new planned communities at Le Val Fourré or Mantes-La-Jolie, closer to the factories. One by one, all the vacant apartments at Les Chamards were rented to foreigners. French residents and "well-integrated" foreigners moved out as soon as they could. French tenants in the towers were followed by Algerians, Moroccans, and Turks, successively, and today by Pakistanis working in the textile industry in Paris. The turnover rate is high: although there are some tenants who have been in Les Chamards for twenty years and cannot imagine moving, 52 percent of all residents in 1989 had arrived since 1984. For schoolteachers in the district it was dizzying: the faces in their classes were constantly changing.

In 1990 all 188 apartments in the so-called little towers were occupied by foreign families. The last French family, the Carrés, moved out in January of that year. After fighting for years for improved living conditions and tenants' rights, they decided to leave. Neither the mayor nor the prefect proved capable of grasping the seriousness of the problem or of stopping the decay in the project. On the pretext that the complex was privately owned, city hall refused to do anything about the deteriorating condition of the buildings, particularly since the residents were all foreigners. In 1988, after the private owners allowed large bills to go unpaid, city officials even allowed the water and electricity to be cut off for several days (though water was supplied under municipal license and electricity by a municipal power authority). If the foreigners were unhappy, they could always leave. It was not until national leaders of the antiracist group SOS–Racisme came down from Paris, bringing with them television crews ready to tape families without water, electricity, or heat, that the national government released funds to pay the bills and put an end to the scandal.

Then, under pressure from the national government, the Dreux Public Housing Authority decided to buy the complex and renovate it. It was only then, with a solution finally in sight, that the Carrés decided to leave. Even then, M. Carré, a retired policeman well versed in trade-union struggles, continued to visit Les Chamards frequently to encourage his former comrades of all nationalities to carry on the fight for the rehabilitation of the project. His son was asked by the tenants' union to resume his post as head of their organization when the residents of two towers were summarily asked to leave in order to allow rehabilitation work to begin, without any guarantee that they would get their old apartments back when the work was finished.

The 608 apartments in the other part of the complex, the "tall towers," were managed by another company, the Azur Group. Rents here were higher, conditions less deplorable. There were 175 foreign families living alongside 433 French families. Among the latter were a large number of retirees from Paris and its suburbs, people who had moved to Dreux quite recently, drawn not only by the Azur's advertisements but also by rents much lower than any to be found in the Paris area. So, in addition to foreigners, there were many recently uprooted French families, forced for financial reasons to leave their old communities. Suddenly they found themselves in a place without a "soul." True, from their tenth- or fifteenth-floor apartments they had the view of the countryside promised in the ads. But when they came down from their towers, they found themselves in parking lots full of unemployed foreign youths. In my conversations with tenants, the obtrusive presence of these youths came up frequently; these juveniles, many charged, were insolent and uncivil. Yet all agreed that some were decent and that the reason why children and teenagers gathered in the hallways and staircases was that there was nowhere else for them to go. One focal point of tension was the grocery store at Les Chamards, which was run by a Muslim who refused to carry ham. Small details like this often take on unsuspected importance in neighborhood conflicts.

One additional point needs emphasizing: Les Chamards had no church. None of the planners had foreseen the need, so nobody had asked for a church. In 1983, however, a mosque was established in a storefront in the complex's shopping center owned by a Moroccan butcher, who chose to make the space available to his fellow Muslims as a house of worship. Its location was marked by a sort of mini-minaret. Many of the retirees who had recently arrived in Dreux themselves were of the Christian faith, and they could not help noticing that a small crowd of Muslim men gathered every Friday in the courtyard at the foot of the high-rises in which they lived. Islam, of course, was much in the news, and reports on the rise of Islamic fundamentalism gave rise to the idea that such congregations might somehow be dangerous. For some, the fact that no pork could be purchased in the neighborhood was proof that this time the Muslim invaders had not been turned back at Poitiers, that now they were running things within shouting distance of the very capital of France. The National Front exploited these feelings. The party's candidate, Marie-France Stirbois, listened to the complaints with a mixture of sympathy, outrage, and amusement and assured worried French citizens of her support: once she was in charge, she promised, she would do everything in her power to get rid of the mosque.

Abandoned Neighborhoods

For forty years, each new housing project was designed to meet the needs of a typical tenant defined in terms of social class, occupation, and income level. The community felt an obligation to provide each of its citizens with shelter, and it met that obligation. Under the roof of each shelter, however, there were differences. Some offered central heating and charged higher rents; others had no central heating and the rent was lower. Some buildings housed foreigners, and people felt that it was right and proper to offer apartments in those same buildings to other foreigners. Some buildings housed people with "antisocial" tendencies, and therefore it was all right to load them up with others of similar ilk. Such was the guiding philosophy of those responsible for urban development, zoning, and public housing.

Over a period of three or four decades such policies, combined with Dreux's chaotic growth, created a city segregated by age, social class, and regional and national origin. In central Dreux fancy apartment buildings sprang up to fill the sites left vacant by the Facel plant and the foundry. Moving outward from the center along a north-south axis, you pass through the old projects of detached, single-family homes built during the tenure of Maurice Viollette. Here the residents are relatively old and have lived in the same house for a long time. Some are skilled blue-collar workers or white-collar employees, many of them in retirement. The majority are French and belong to families that have lived in Dreux for at least two generations. Moving still farther out from the center, you encounter buildings that seem to have been scattered here and there with no particular logic. You become lost in a maze of access ways that are not really streets, even though they have street names. Some of the buildings look shabby; others, repainted more recently, are less depressing. There are few trees or parks or gardens and no cafés or restaurants. Nor are there any streetcorners that seem like inviting places for neighbors to pause for a chat about the weather or the day's events. On the other hand, you see plenty of idle youths loitering around the high-rises.

The new housing projects are poorly laid out, uninspiring in design, and shabbily constructed. The lack of thermal and sound insulation in apartment walls, the dearth of shopping facilities in residential neighborhoods, and the lack of attention to the environment have permanently altered the character of life in Dreux. The harm done to the city during the time when large numbers of new housing units had to be built quickly has still not been repaired, not by a long shot. In December 1989 television viewers across France were horrified to learn that people in Romania could not heat their apartments above 56 degrees. On the eve of my election in 1977, I was horrified to discover that there were infants living in Dreux where apartments could not be heated above 50 degrees in the middle of winter. From the outside it was impossible to tell: the facades of those buildings were reassuring.

In 1982 Dreux was one of sixteen cities in France to receive substantial funding from the national government for the purpose of rehabilitating decayed urban areas. The goal was not simply to renovate buildings, paint stairwells, and repair broken mailboxes. Hubert Dubedout, the head of this new program, saw it as a way of mobilizing local officials, bureaucrats, organizations, and tenants so as to establish first a dialogue and then a genuine community with respect for the individual dignity. To change the image of a neighborhood, it was not enough to install a few flowerboxes along sidewalks or to repaint gray facades pink or blue. Decay affected more than housing: unemployment, boredom, noise, crime, drugs—all of these maladies were intertwined. To get to the bottom of the discontent, feelings of insecurity, and tension between families and generations, one has to identify social, economic, and cultural needs that are not always articulately expressed. "Where there is ugliness, there is no democracy. When things are rotten, democracy goes out the window," according to the architect Roland Castro.[7] He is no doubt right. But patching up crumbling plaster is a superficial response that fails to change people's lives in fundamental ways. If beauty alone were a sufficient foundation for democracy, solutions would be fairly simple. But it will take understanding and imagination to restore (or perhaps to establish) a social life in a neighborhood where, over the past twenty or thirty years, the accidents of history, economics, and chance have brought together men and women with vastly different outlooks and expectations. It is possible to spend millions and accomplish nothing if planners fail to pay attention to the needs of children, if they fail to provide pleasant places for adults to congregate, if they fail to provide teenagers with places to meet other than basements and apartment lobbies and things to do other than shout insults at elderly retirees and janitors.

Planning cannot solve every problem. After the Lyons riots in 1990, Roland Castro called for the creation of a Ministry of Cities, but such a step would merely add an additional bureaucracy to the ones that already exist. It is hard to see in any case what such an agency could do about youths left idle by the scarcity of jobs. Rehabilitated neighborhoods and fine architecture can hardly be expected to calm the rage they feel at being excluded from society. One more government agency is not what they need to give them a sense of future possibility.

Some positive results can be achieved, however, and work done over the past ten years has begun to yield fruit. Le Val Fourré in Mantes-la-Jolie, Les Minguettes in Vénissieux, and the "Four Thousand Complex" at La Courneuve were the hot spots of the early 1980s, far more troubled than Les Chamards in Dreux. Today, although the equilibrium may remain fragile, these former hot spots are in the news as models of successful rehabilitation made possible by a genuine partnership among elected officials, bureaucrats, and local organizations. Of course outbreaks of violence will occur as long as people continue to be excluded from full participation in society. Although such crises are not necessarily signs of failure, they do signal problems still in need of attention. Standing in front of the hulks of burned automobiles, the mayor of Vaulx-en-Velin declared that he was not about to give up. What had been destroyed would be repaired, and quickly. But the most important need was to understand what had happened in order to eradicate the causes of destructive rage, to head off trouble before it happened.

In Dreux, by contrast, the regional newspapers have reported on the continuing deterioration of the situation owing to the absence of local political leadership. The last two days of Ramadan (the month-long Muslim holiday) in the spring of 1989 were a feverish time. On the southern heights, the city's most populous and most "immigrant" section, gangs of teenagers and children staged their own *intifada:* cars were stoned, the mall was looted. Fortunately a rainstorm cooled things down. The remainder of the summer witnessed a number of scuffles, and police vehicles were regularly targeted. Since then there have been countless incidents. The mall—the area's only attraction—has been a focal point of violence. Hardly a week goes by without some incident, echoes of which reverberate in the local press. The mall has hired additional security guards. Storeowners have organized to defend themselves. Policemen ride the buses that serve the dangerous parts of town.

There are fewer and fewer organizations dedicated to keeping the social fabric intact. City hall, hunkered down in the center of town, and the national bureaucracy, hamstrung by red tape, have failed to heed the call for help of men and women in trouble. More than that, officials are actually afraid of those calls for help and would rather silence them. The spirit of cooperation and dialogue that surfaced briefly during Mitterrand's first term as president has long since vanished. The Priority Education Zones established by former education minister Alain Savary, the job-training programs promoted by Bertrand Schwartz, the juvenile crime-prevention program and the program to substitute public works for prison terms advocated by Gilbert Bonnemaison have all fizzled out.

To include training programs in the minimum-income legislation might have helped the unemployed get back on their feet. Strangely, however, the government of Michel Rocard, which might have been expected to take a new approach to government

71

intervention, chose deconcentration over decentralization. In plain language, this meant giving power to bureaucrats rather than to elected officials and community groups. Except in places where local officials were still enthusiastic enough to muster sufficient energy to resist the bureaucrats' recapture of authority that they had been forced to share after Mitterrand's election in 1981, the regression that began in 1986 continued under Rocard. His idea of "relying on civil society" was to bring people without experience of political life and its pitfalls into government. In practice, though, whatever could be recentralized was recentralized. The experimental approaches tried early in Mitterrand's first term, in which people likely to be affected by government decisions were consulted in the decisionmaking process, were dropped. The bureaucracy reverted to old habits, and French bureaucrats have never looked kindly on negotiation, cooperation, or innovation. What they know is rules, priorities written down on a piece of paper, executive orders and ministerial memoranda they interpret as they see fit.

Many political activists simply tired of the constant bureaucratic infighting and gave up. Those who hung on were often dismayed to find themselves characterized as troublemakers by senior officials, even though they thought they were supporting the government's own objectives. The minute a local activist raised a demand or submitted a modest proposal, he or she was summoned before the subprefect and warned that for the government to respond favorably would be to play into the hands of the National Front. Teachers, meanwhile, no longer vied for a posting to Dreux. Recent graduates and relatively inexperienced teachers were sent to the most difficult schools, and the instant they arrived they applied for a transfer. Some resigned altogether.

New Forms of Urban Pathology

All those young people who, if rumor is to be believed, sow terror in the city—where do they come from? Les Chamards? The apartment complex at La Croix Tiennac? The high-rises are not the only sources of misery, which is the mother of boredom and delinquency. Many people who work in Poissy, Trappes, and Paris share the same dream: to own a home of their own. Land in Dreux is less expensive than in the suburbs of Paris. Real-estate developers sold illusory hopes. As a result, there are people who own homes in Dreux who spend only a few hours a day there. Husband and wife both set out for work at dawn, to travel 70 miles, and return home late at night. It takes two incomes to keep up the house payments, and since there is no work to be had in Dreux, both must travel to Paris. The children remain home, left to their own devices all day long.

Much has been written about housing projects for the poor, from Sarcelles to northern Marseilles, from Monfermeil to Dreux. Much less has been written about the developments of single-family homes that are like villages incorporated within the city limits or attached to existing rural communities. Yet these places breed new and insidious urban pathologies. Pierre Bourdieu has shown what lies hidden behind the facades of these small suburban homes, describing how the purchase of a house is "one of the major causes of lower-middle-class poverty, or, rather, of all the petty miseries, all the injuries to freedom, hope, and desire, which burden life with cares, disappointments, limitations, failures, and, almost inevitably, depression and resentment as well." Rightly he notes that "this wretched yet triumphant 'populace' in no way resembles the populist illusion of what 'the people' are like. At once too near and too distant, such people draw nothing but sarcastic and disapproving remarks from intellectuals, who deplore their 'bourgeoisification' and are critical of their misguided aspirations and equally misguided and foolish pleasures. All of this is condensed in the attack on the myth of the single-family home."[8]

As you wander through the heights of Dreux between high-rise apartment complexes or on the outskirts of town, you come across the developments: streets as straight as a die lined with new small homes, each with its fenced-in yard and watchdog. Over the past fifteen years, many such standardized homes have been built in the empty spaces between apartment projects (interstices referred to as "missing teeth" in the jargon of city planners). The idea was to prevent nearby villages from pulling away residents of Dreux who wanted to have their own homes. The developments are full of blue-collar workers and middle managers who, along with the joys of individual ownership, have discovered the anxieties of making monthly mortgage payments. If they fail to keep up, the bank can attach their wages, thus alerting the employer to the employee's indebtedness. If a worker is laid off, the consequences are dramatic. Every time you pass a boarded-up home with a sign announcing a foreclosure sale, you can be sure that another family has met with tragedy: unemployment has put an end to many a dream and sent many a one-time homeowner back into the projects.

Who are the role models for the young toughs about whom the papers write every day? Their own older brothers or the brothers of their friends. At age seventeen or eighteen, schooling becomes unavailable. Young people then find themselves on the streets without work, a burden on parents who more often than not blame the youngsters for their own failure. At the start of the schoolyear in 1990, some fifty junior-high-school students were deemed "too old" or "too difficult" to continue in school. The high schools refused to take them because they lacked the necessary prerequisites. Those fifty teenagers joined the ranks of others who had been rejected in previous years. The following fall another crop of teenagers would be added to their ranks.[9] At their parents' urging, a few would seek help from the local "social-service mission."[10] With a little luck they might be offered a place in a job-training program. Here too, however, the bureaucracy jealously guarded its prerogatives. Since the national government was paying for this job training, the bureaucrats intended to remain firmly in control. Private groups that tried to offer continuing education received little or nothing in the way of subsidies. The Ministry of National Education gobbled up most of the avilable funds for its own continuing education department (called GRETA, an acronym for Groupement d'Etablissements). Thus many of the same youths who had been expelled from the regular schools found themselves enrolled in training programs set up in the same schools that also symbolized their failure, taught by the same teachers who had expelled them a few months earlier but who now discovered they could earn a few extra francs by taking on the additional chore of occupational training. (For the ministry, these salary supplements for teachers proved to be a useful way of relieving pressure for higher teachers' salaries in general.)

For young men caught in this situation, there was little prospect other than trips to the employment agency and hanging out in the parking lots. (For girls it was different: many of them studied harder in the hope that success in school would offer a way out.) In the absence of local organizations or municipal programs capable of standing in for absent or powerless parents, these boys were left to fend for themselves. They joined gangs and followed leaders reputed for boldness in challenging the police. The police themselves lacked the means to respond and often felt helpless. What could be done about young rock throwers, window breakers, motorcycle and car thieves, many of them only twelve or thirteen years old? One policeman revealed that he had "just arrested a French kid, age sixteen and a half, with 300 robberies to his credit. What are we supposed to do with him? Throw him in jail? The prison system isn't set up for this kind of criminal."[11] Law-enforcement agencies are asked to deal with the effects of a situation whose causes no one is willing to treat. Hiring more policemen—the solution advocated by all parties, from the left to the National Front—does nothing but pacify the general public. The antisocial, disturbing behavior of the young is merely the symptom of a malady that is far more profound.

At the conclusion of our tour of Dreux—avoiding the usual tourist sights—it is obvious that Dreux does not exist. The city consists of twenty separate districts containing twenty distinct and separate populations. There is no community, only a collection of people who are strangers to one another and whose numbers are growing.

France Closes Its Borders (1974)

Where did all those immigrants—whom the mayor in 1971 already considered too numerous—come from? As early as 1950 they began arriving with their cardboard suitcases to run the assembly plants and build the new sections of town. By 1954 they accounted for 1.4 percent of the population; by 1968, 7 percent; and by 1970, more than 10 percent. In the Dreux-Vernouillet area the 1971 census reported 3,622 foreigners of thirty-one different nationalities.[12] Most numerous were the Portuguese (975), followed by Spaniards (774), Moroccans (544), Algerians (443), and Italians (362). There were also 147 Tunisians and 120 Yugoslavians but only 22 Turks, and not a single person from Pakistan, Mali, or Zaire.

In 1974, when the government decided to close France's borders in response to growing unemployment nationwide, there were 5,623 foreigners in the Dreux-Vernouillet area. The distress call issued by the mayor in 1971 failed to stem the tide: in four years, from 1970 to 1974, the number of foreigners increased by 55 percent. During that brief period, the nationality structure of the foreign population also changed dramatically. The Portuguese still formed the largest group; their number increased by 70 percent. But the number of Moroccans increased by 160 percent, and the size of the Algerian and Tunisian contingents also rose sharply (82 and 80 percent respectively). Meanwhile the number of Spaniards and Italians decreased. What happened in the four years leading up to the closing of France's borders?

A study of Dreux's immigration files for 1973, together with company employment statistics for 1970–1974, yields information necessary for understanding what brought so many foreigners to France. During the period in question, labor-intensive industries in the Dreux area (including machine shops, electronics plants, and construction firms) employed a higher proportion of foreign workers than ever before. Radiotechnique, for example, hired 174 new foreign workers in this period. The Comasec plant, which manufactured rubberized protective clothing, went from 30 foreign workers out of a total of 170 employees in 1970 (17 percent of the work force) to 92 foreign workers out of a total of 389 (30 percent) in 1974. Bourdin et Chaussée, a construction firm founded in 1972 and specializing in public-works projects, exemplifies the reliance of firms in this sector (quite active at the time) on foreign workers: of the 119 workers it employed in 1974, 64, or nearly 54 percent, were foreigners.

The records also make it clear that Dreux was not only a city in which immigrants were recruited by local firms hungry for unskilled labor but also a bedroom community for workers employed in the Paris region and, to a lesser extent, throughout the Eure-et-Loir département. This was particularly true of foreign workers. In 1973, 424 of Dreux's immigrants were employed outside the Dreux area. Records pertaining to Moroccan immigrants are particularly illuminating in this regard. Census data indicate that 738 Moroccans (men, women, and children) lived in the city at the time. Of these, 163 were employed outside the Dreux area. Of that group, 40 worked in the département, most of them at one factory in Nogent-le-Roi, about 12 miles from Dreux. The rest worked in the Paris area, largely in the automobile industry: at the Simca and Chrysler plants in Poissy, at Renault plants in Flins and Aubergenville, or at Fiat Unic in Trappes. The same study for 1973 also shows that 602 foreign workers (out of some 3,000 adults listed in census figures) were housed in dormitories built for them by their employers: Radiotechnique, Bourdin et Chaussée, and Sonacotra. These were single men living in deplorable conditions: one police report mentions that Portuguese, Moroccan, and Turkish construction workers were packed into tiny wooden bungalows filled with bunk beds and equipped with a single wash basin without running water. Workers accompanied by their families lived in privately owned apartments. Those who came from Latin countries (Spain, Portugal, Italy) lived in old Dreux, while the more recent immigrants from North Africa and Turkey found apartments at Les Chamards and, to a lesser extent, in the projects of Dreux and Vernouillet.

In 1974 the bulk of the foreign population was still male. Only 33.5 percent of Dreux's foreign residents were adult females. Yet the presence of family units—the first sign of an intention to remain for an extended period on French soil—became noticeable among non-European immigrants. Among European immigrants, who had been in France longer, the proportion of families was already high: 43 percent of the Spanish community was female, for example, and 40 percent of of the Portuguese community. Meanwhile, the Moroccan population was 63 percent male, and the Turkish population 83 percent male.

Still More Foreigners

Every French government since 1974 has insisted that the borders are now closed. It was easy for citizens to believe that foreigners would no longer be allowed to enter France, just as they had long believed that the foreigners already in the country would one day return "home." The government even instituted a well-publicized program of subsidies to encourage unneeded foreign workers to return to their native lands.[13] Nevertheless, on 1 January 1990, nearly sixteen years after the closing of the borders, there were 11,573 foreigners living in the Dreux area, or nearly double the number living there in 1975. The number of nationalities represented also more than doubled: 67 as opposed to 31. The largest group was now the Moroccans (4,870), followed by the Turks (1,915) and the Portuguese (1,535). The number of Algerians had receded to its 1973 level (660) after reaching a maximum of 1,510 in 1980. There were 547 Tunisians, well ahead of the Spanish, who now numbered only 170. And while Italians still outnumbered Pakistanis, the number of the latter had increased spectacularly, from 2 in 1974 to 302 at the beginning of 1990.

Behind the population figures we see a remarkable demographic change. In 1970 local people worried that the foreign population consisted mainly of single men. Cut off from home and roots, such men, it was whispered, were potentially dangerous, vulnerable to alcoholism, and a threat to French women. By 1990, however, the chief complaint against the foreigners was their children. Although men are still proportionately overrepresented in the foreign population, the composition of that population increasingly resembles that of the native population, and natives are especially irritated by the number of children and teenagers of foreign extraction. The young people are a problem in the schools and a problem in the housing projects and neighborhoods. Many French homeowners, still paying for their new homes, left their old apartments because they had so many problems with North African families. The North Africans tended to have large families, and the overcrowding gave the projects—and therefore all the tenants—a bad image. Anxious to leave, French tenants succumbed to the allure of developers' advertising, which reminded them of the "special importance attached to a home's symbolic value."[14] They dreamed of the kind of life depicted in the ads, surrounded by happy children and neighbors of their own kind. In the single-family development, however, they found still more Arabs, and those Arabs often owned larger homes because the housing subsidy they received was based on the number of dependent children.

Between 1975 and 1982 the population of Dreux stopped growing for the first time since the turn of the century. People had begun to move out: all told, some 3,900 people left during this seven-year period. Both French residents and foreigners were among those leaving, but to unequal degrees. Both groups were also represented among new arrivals, but foreigners outnumbered French: "Between 1975 and 1982," according to the economist Paul Bachelard, "Dreux witnessed a decline in its French population of 1,395 and an increase of its foreign population of 2,050 [as a result of families being reunited as well as new births]. As a result, the proportion of foreigners in the population rose from 15 percent in 1975 to 20.8 percent in 1982, with a very uneven distribution across the city's neighborhoods. Between one census and the next, the proportion of foreigners rose from 7.5 to 9.3 percent in the valley, from 10.4 to 12.7 percent on the northern heights, and from 20.4 to 31.2 percent on the southern heights, where foreigners made up 60 percent of the residents of Les Chamards in 1984."[15]

The barracks that local companies built to house their workers now stood empty and had to be converted to other uses. Foreign workers, reunited with their families, began to integrate. Many now lived in apartments or single-family homes. There were homeowners as well as tenants among them. They were no longer confined to "reserved quarters." It is misleading, by the way, to speak of "ethnic ghettos." Some neighborhoods did have high concentrations of foreign residents, but "immigrant" is not an ethnic group. At Les Chamards, for example, Algerians, Moroccans, Turks, Pakistanis, and others share the same high-rises.

Gérard Noiriel notes that "while politicians in favor of assimilation continually called attention to the danger of 'national groupings' and repeatedly recommended 'disseminating' newcomers throughout the country, the nation's overriding economic interests led to precisely the opposite outcome."[16] This general remark can be applied to Dreux. The automobile manufacturers of the Seine valley, always on the lookout for low-cost housing, had a common interest with the real-estate developers who owned Les Chamards. Foreign workers did not object to this solution, for immigrants are always keen to live together in groups in order to protect one another from the hostility of the natives and to keep alive memories of the homeland. "After some years of seasonal migration," Noiriel continues, "an initial group of immigrants decides to settle in one place. These pioneers then bring others from their own families or villages back home. Within a few years, a veritable community may spring into being, and that community may survive for decades, replenishing its ranks from the same original sources."

This phenomenon can also be seen at work in Dreux. One social worker, himself of Turkish origin, recounts how Turks found one another in the early 1970s: "One man employed by Simca at Poissy found an apartment at Les Chamards through the firm's internal advertising. After becoming friendly with the caretaker of one of the towers, he began asking the man to help him find apartments for his Turkish coworkers, in return for which they were willing to offer 'small gifts.' The practice proved successful, and many Simca workers moved into Les Chamards and before long were inviting their wives to come live with them."[17] This self-recruitment network ensured that most of the Turks moving into Les Chamards came from two or three Anatolian villages. In 1985 Pakistanis began moving in thanks to a similar process. Thirty years earlier, many Bretons had come to Dreux from the same part of Brittany and had colonized a couple of the city's neighborhoods before fanning out through the area.

Completely occupied by foreigners, Les Chamards' smaller towers functioned in a sense as portals into French society. For twenty-five years they were an entry point, with a tenant turnover of 10 to 15 percent annually. Other projects on the heights, in which a majority of the tenants are French, are less talked about: they do not make as strong an impression on the imagination as do projects or neighborhoods in which everybody is a foreigner. Sociologically, however, they are not very different: they are poverty ghettos in which French people live alongside assimilated and new immigrants. These places are the result of geographic mobility during the years of economic growth. The people who live in them came from other parts of France, other countries, or other continents. Nearly all of them uprooted themselves in the hope of social advancement. Now poverty, a shortage of jobs, and the lack of skills have turned them into virtual prisoners in their own homes. It is not like the old days, when the police had to keep an eye on ex-convicts to make sure they did not violate the terms of their release. Dreux is the place in which they work or collect unemployment checks. As they watch the world changing around them on their television screens every night, their inability to ease their plight becomes that much more unbearable.

The Influx Continues

Although the present mayor, Jean Hieaux of the RPR, contends that he made no promises about immigration in 1983, voters at the time remember reading in their newspapers that the election of a right-wing mayor would surely reverse the influx of immigrants into Dreux. In any case, there was no mistaking the raucous rhetoric of Hieaux's allies in the National Front. Jean-Pierre Stirbois repeatedly stated in the media that, with him in city hall, immigration would decline. Stirbois served as assistant to the mayor from 1983 to 1988, and throughout those years the number of foreigners in Dreux continued to increase. Shrewdly, the National Front salvaged its image by blaming the mayor's "weakness." Hieaux reacted by blaming the policies of left-wing governments at the national level. This explanation enjoyed substantial popular support, but it also redounded to the benefit of the National Front. In fact, neither the mayor's alleged weakness nor the government's policies concerning immigration and residence can account for the fact that, since Hieaux assumed office, the number of foreigners in Dreux has increased by 10 percent.

The first reason for the increase is that foreigners, like Frenchmen, have children. Although the fertility rate for foreign women living in France increasingly approximates that of French women, it remains higher, especially among first-generation immigrants. Recently arrived immigrants are still sending for their families, moreover. Since 1984 the regulations have been tightened considerably, not to say turned into a bureaucratic obstacle course: the worker who wants to bring his wife and children into the country must show that he has a large enough apartment to accommodate them, but in order to obtain a large apartment in a public housing project he must prove that his family is already living in France.

Furthermore, foreigners bring more foreigners—and not merely the wives and children of those already present. Dreux, long a city of immigration, is in contact with many parts of the world in which France is seen as a kind of paradise. To people who are hungry or forbidden to speak their own language or to worship as they choose, to young people who aspire to live the life they see in movies and television, Dreux is a place to escape to, and they save their money for just that. They may know a relative there or a friend or the friend of a friend. Some come with tourist visas, others risk crossing the border illegally into what for them is the "land of the rights of man." Of course those who come illegally may well find themselves being escorted onto an airplane a few years later.

This was how many Turks found their way to Dreux. The origins of the Turkish community appear to have been connected with the Comasec corporation, which in the 1970s recruited workers from Turkey for particularly unpleasant work that French workers were unwilling to do for the wages offered. The first group of these workers, which included some Kurds, formed the core of the Turkish community. The Kurds, having established a foothold, helped bring other members of the same ethnic group, all opponents of the Turkish regime, to France. They crossed the border illegally but once inside France asked for political asylum and were issued temporary papers. Kurds already established in Dreux then took the new arrivals into their homes. Until the Office of Refugees issued its decision, these candidates for asylum enjoyed full legal status. If they could prove that they deserved refugee status under the terms of the Geneva Convention, they were allowed to remain in France. If not, an expulsion order would be issued.

Although most applications for asylum were filed by Turks, they were not alone. Every now and then the local press printed an article about an immigrant who was expelled for failing to prove that he was in danger in his native land from something other than hunger or an aversion to the regime in power. Take, for example, Judoka, a native of Zaire well known to inhabitants of Dreux's southern heights. Chosen by Zaire authorities to compete in the

Olympic Games, he discovered the charms of freedom during his travels. He had no difficulty finding a job with a security firm in Paris, which sent him to work in Dreux as a patrolman in one of the local malls. In March 1990 his neighbors learned from the morning papers that he had been arrested and taken to Orly airport, where he was put on a plane headed for Zaire.

But new births, reunited families, and the influx of refugees do not by themselves account for the steady increase in the number of foreigners in Dreux. Another important factor is the availability of very low-cost housing in buildings whose French tenants have moved out owing to dilapidated conditions. At Les Chamards, for example, a Pakistani community has replaced the old Turkish community. Employees of the Sentier corporation, these Pakistanis were unable to find housing in Paris or its suburbs. In Dreux, however, they discovered empty apartments at low rents less than an hour by train from the capital. An information network developed: the moment an apartment was vacated, a Pakistani family appeared to claim it. The firm that managed the building in 1984–85 made no bones about its eagerness to rent to Pakistani tenants, who always paid their rent on time. The same thing happened at Le Murger, a private apartment complex originally occupied by French tenants exclusively but gradually taken over by Turks. The rental agent assured the owners that Turkish tenants would cause no problems, and in any case if there were problems it was easier to get rid of troublesome foreigners than French tenants. As it turned out, though, the influx of Turks damaged the image of the apartment complex, and rents fell. The buildings were then sold at a bargain price, and the apartments were rented out to foreigners.

Thus a part of the increase in Dreux's foreign population was due not to continued immigration from abroad but to population shifts within France's borders. Some officials even tried to unload "problem" foreigners on Dreux, as shown by an incident that occurred in January 1990. The police chief of Les Yvelines was called on to deal with a disturbance in a Kurdish workers' barracks in Poissy. His solution was to seek other housing for those deemed troublemakers. Upon learning that thirty rooms were available in the Sonacotra workers' barracks in Dreux, he had the Kurds transported there in military vehicles, without even informing the prefect of Eure-et-Loir. Although the whole operation was carried out with the utmost discretion, news of the move traveled faster than the army's trucks. No sooner had the Kurds arrived than they were met by other policemen acting on the prefect's orders. They were taken to Dreux's railway station and placed aboard the first train for Paris.

Foreigners, Immigrants, People of Dreux

Statistics on the number of foreigners in France are compiled annually (although illegal aliens of course go uncounted). But how many of Dreux's citizens with French nationality are actually foreign-born? The March 1990 census figures should provide a basis for answering this question because the census takers asked about the national origins of French citizens. As of this writing, the figures have not been released, although unsubstantiated numbers are frequently bandied about. "Don't be hypocritical," one city councillor insisted. "You have to count the 30 percent of the population that came from North Africa with French citizenship. The fact is that 60 percent of our population comes from outside metropolitan France."[18] True or false? The census will settle the matter. But in the meantime we can notice how easy it is for politicians to produce a new category of citizens like a rabbit out of a hat: suddenly we are confronted with "non-metropolitans."

Behind the numbers lie the countless threads from which our national history is woven: yesterday's foreigners have disappeared into France's melting pot, yet not everyone thinks that genuine French fare will emerge. The number of Italians and Spaniards listed in the census figures has decreased steadily since 1970. The number of Portuguese peaked in the early 1980s and then dropped precipitously. Did all the Italians, Portuguese, and Spaniards who disappeared from the census tables return to their native lands? The statistics fail to tell the full story. Some did indeed return home. But many became naturalized citizens of France and are no longer required to file as aliens with the prefecture. Many people of North African extraction now possess French identity cards, and not all are *harkis*. The children of Algerians, Moroccans, Tunisians, and Turks born in Dreux are French citizens. The oldest children, those who arrived in France as infants, could not claim citizenship by virtue of the so-called *jus soli* (which ties citizenship to place of birth rather than blood), unless they happened to be Algerian.[19] Knowing that their future lay in France, however, many of them applied for naturalization. In the older generation, applications for asylum were relatively rare because many still dreamed of returning home one day. Yet in the end the elderly also stayed on so as not to lose touch with their grandchildren, whose homeland was now Dreux, in France. All they asked was that they be laid to rest in their native soil on the other side of the Mediterranean.

Today, when you knock on the door of an apartment bearing a Portuguese or North African name, you are apt to find people of more than one nationality living together under the same roof. The parents are generally still citizens of their native country. Older children may be of either nationality, while younger children are usually French. Raising the question of nationality is likely to trigger a debate within the family, rubbing salt on a wound that only time can heal. The real generation gap depends not on age but on memory of the country of origin: the children most alienated from their parents are the ones who, born in France, know no other home. Older children, born in their parents' homeland, retain strong emotional ties to their birthplace and attach considerable symbolic importance to the question of nationality. Take, for example, the president of the Portuguese Association of Dreux. At age thirty he has no intention of becoming a French citizen. He wants to be accepted as he is, with the papers he already has. He knows that his children will probably be French and will most likely live in Dreux. He himself feels that Dreux is his home. But he doesn't want to forget that he is Portuguese, and he doesn't want anyone else to forget either.

A child born in Dreux to foreign parents can, upon reaching the age of majority, apply at the local courthouse for a certificate of nationality. Then, armed with this document, he or she can obtain an identity card from the subprefecture. To many people, French nationality means nothing more than the right to possess this yellow card, as it is popularly known. Times have changed since the 1930s, when, as the actress Simone Signoret recounts in her novel *Adieu Volodia,* central European Jews eagerly passed around their precious French citizenship papers for all to admire—those papers signified acceptance into a nation that was said to be the cradle of enlightenment, revolution, and democracy. For today's youths, citizenship is not a matter of deep emotion but a license to thumb their noses at authority: "I've got my yellow card," they say, "so now you can't kick me out for fooling around."

Can we blame them for equating French citizenship with a mere piece of paper? These are, after all, people who were born in France. They are products of republican schools. Kadder, whose Algerian father has worked at Radiotechnique for a quarter of a century, lives on the same floor as Roberto, the son of a Portuguese mason, and Pascal, whose parents work on the assembly line at Nomel. They grew up together as children and hung out as adolescents. Kadder, in no hurry to pick up his identity card, finally did apply for one when he realized that he might be expelled from France on the slightest pretext. He knew all about Algeria from having visited there on a tour with other young people from the neighborhood. Before that trip, when people called him a foreigner, he used to say that one day he would return to his homeland. He no longer believes that, for in Algeria too he discovered that he was considered a foreigner because he cannot speak Arabic. "Anyway," he adds with a smile, "there are no pinball machines in Algiers."

*　　*　　*

In regard to choosing a nationality, the year 1986 seems to have been a turning point. French-born children of foreign parents who had been reluctant to apply for the yellow card now did what they had to do to obtain French citizenship. Those who hurried to the courthouse in 1986 had been adolescents in 1983, the year in which virulent xenophobic sentiments surfaced in the campaign for mayor of Dreux. Spray-painted slogans had appeared on walls: "France for the French!" "Arabs out!" "Le Pen Now!" And in 1986 a right-wing majority in the National Assembly forced Socialist president François Mitterrand to "cohabit" with Jacques Chirac, the leader of the right, as prime minister. The new government's commitment to "the defense of French identity" and revision of the Code of Nationality made the yellow card indispensable. Young people felt less vulnerable if they had papers to produce on demand.

When one passes a "foreign-looking" man in the streets of Dreux, how is one to guess the color of his passport? Such encounters do take place, for the two societies—that of the city and that of the heights—can no longer ignore each other. First-generation immigrants did not often venture into the center of town, but their children are not so fearful, cautious, or reluctant. Nor do they feel out of place. The Grande Rue between the bell-tower and the Billy crossroads is one of their favorite haunts. They feel at home in central Dreux. But to the oldtimers it makes no difference whether these youths have yellow cards or not, for their names are Kadder and Mouloud and they look Mediterranean. Hence they are labeled "immigrant" or even "illegitimate."[20]

A visitor to Dreux finds innumerable signs of what people call "the immigration." To judge by physical appearance and clothing, one would say that North Africans and Turks account for far more than the 28 percent of the population reported in 1990 statistics. In Dreux, a French city located at the juncture of Ile-de-France, Normandy, and the Beauce, the streets are filled with "Mediterranean types." The newcomers have joined the city, even if the city has not yet entirely accepted them.

As Dreux Goes, So Goes France

What happened to the Dreux once known to its natives, to those who were there before? In order to answer this question, we have to determine what is meant by "natives" and "before." Some Dreux voters greeted the National Front's success in the 1983 elections with triumphant cries of "Dreux for the Drouais!" Others—generally people of the left—responded with shouts of "Stirbois back to Neuilly!"[21] To the National Front's supporters, Drouais was synonymous with French. To their opponents on the left, a Drouais was first and foremost a resident of Dreux: Jean-Pierre Stirbois, the National Front's successful candidate, was a carpetbagger, unwelcome in Dreux.

As we have seen, it was in 1954 that the population of Dreux began its explosive increase. It would be interesting to know what became of the 16,818 people living in Dreux that year. How many of them were in the crowd that gathered in front of the dance hall on election night to celebrate or deplore the victory of the National Front?

During the intervening twenty-nine years, many French families had left their farms to settle in the city. Some residents of Dreux left in search of jobs or a better life in other parts of France. Owing to the economic character of the city, young people who obtained higher education generally left Dreux never to return, except for those few whose future was already mapped out: they were expected to take over their father's medical practice or law office. Of the students in my senior class in high school, I am the only one who has remained in Dreux. And remember that my association with the city is unique: if I had not decided to translate my love for Dreux into a political relationship, I would have little reason to visit other than to see my family. Every year hundreds of young people leave Dreux to study in Orléans, Tours, and Rouen. After graduation they are unlikely to find in Dreux the kind of managerial or engineering job they are looking for. Not all of these young people are of French origin. The children of foreigners and *harkis* also leave Dreux for good. One consequence of this is the lament, frequently heard in town, that there are no elites in the foreign communities.

Not all the old Drouais have left, however. Personal memories extend back over generations. Life in the provinces is such that at every streetcorner you are bound to spot a familiar face and linger for a brief conversation. Although many small shops in the center of town have succumbed to competition from the malls, there are still businesses that have been passed down from father to son or daughter. Many of the craftsmen whose workshops line the valley's slopes are the sons of yesterday's craftsmen. My brother the marble cutter is one of them. On the heights, some working-class families have lived in the same neighborhood for generations, and in some cases family members have worked for the same firm. The small town of yesteryear lives on, immersed in the middle-sized city of today. But what does "yesteryear" mean? What does being a citizen of Dreux mean to those who call themselves Drouais? Obviously to be Drouais is to be recognized as such without question. But the criteria of recognition have changed.

Dreux's recent history shows how amnesia operates. Each new wave of immigration erases what went on before. Those who have endured the torment of deracination and experienced the humiliation attendant upon joining a new community are sometimes the first to oppose those who wish in turn to become Drouais. Among Dreux's well-to-do families today, there are surely descendants of the convicts at whom townspeople pointed fingers a century ago. Among the city's elite there are grandchildren of immigrants. One of the leading members of the Junior Chamber of Commerce is named Alain Gabrielli. His grandfather was a refugee from Italian fascism in the 1920s. A mason, the elder Gabrielli turned his strong wrists to advantage and created a construction firm that by 1960 had become the largest in Dreux; yet he still spoke Italian. One also finds the sons and even grandsons of Spanish and Portuguese immigrants among Dreux's executives, entrepreneurs, and merchants, whose immigrant roots are apparent only in their surnames. These descendants of once-denigrated "Dagos" and "Polaks" and "Portos" are so "Drouais" that it is not unusual to find them in the ranks of the extreme right, leading the fight to protect the local "race" against the foreign invader and approvingly citing the words of one local physician, the chairman of the National Front support committee, who in 1983 stated that the time had come to "preserve the city's biological equilibrium."[22] The first step to be taken toward that end was of course to send the immigrants back home.

One of the first proponents of an alliance between the right and the extreme right in Dreux was a man named Toni Serio. From 1983 to 1988 he served as Jean-Pierre Stirbois's right-hand man. People spoke of him as the mayor's heir apparent. He was French—but what about his parents and grandparents? Naturally since he was of Italian extraction, he was considered a "member of the family," as the writer Jean Cau, the historian Pierre Chaunu, and others who share their xenophobic views are fond of saying. The offspring of Italian immigrants who were stoned and beaten at Aigues-Mortes in 1893 are today good Frenchmen, as are the progeny of those refugees from fascism who were branded "unassimilable" in the 1930s.[23] The Arabs are somehow supposed to be different. Yet in the March 1989 municipal elections Abdelkader Hamiche, the son of a *harki*, was elected on a right-wing slate. He opposed granting political rights to foreign residents. The city government was relying on Hamiche to make the point that citizenship and nationality are inseparable and that the price of nationality is to shed blood for your country. This son of a military auxiliary had become a political auxiliary. Who says Abdelkader Hamiche can't be assimilated? On the contrary, he is a perfect example of the assimilation of French values—the most conservative French values. It is as if one way for the "new French" to immigrate is to hide their past, deny their origins, and refuse to allow history to repeat itself for the benefit of those more recently arrived than themselves.

The allusion to shedding blood for your country is an appeal to a common history, which unites the citizens of metropolitan France with the citizens of France's overseas départements and the subjects of its colonies. In peacetime, however, French racists do not always make distinctions between foreigners who have served the French nation and those who have not: the children of *harkis* and Moroccans as well as Algerians have been victims of murderous violence in Roanne, Saint-Florentin, and elsewhere. The fathers and grandfathers of many of those same young victims fought for France at Verdun or Monte Cassino. For Abdelkader Hamiche, apparently, history began in 1954 and ended in 1962. But the real history of France and its foreigners is far longer and more complex, as well as more painful. Today's blood and tears are no less tragic than yesterday's.

Dreux, like the rest of France, is a melting pot in which it takes time for the old and the new to mix. With each new generation of immigrants, some from the previous generation have tried to make the newcomers pay dearly for every advantage they might receive. They succeeded only in slowing down what is sometimes cautiously referred to as integration but is in fact assimilation into the French nation. In order to justify their attitude, they accentuate a difference—skin color, foreign appearance, a foreign-sounding last name, religion—and cite it as grounds for incompatibility. In so doing they force the most recent arrivals to retreat into their own communities. After every election campaign, during which politicians of the right and extreme right regularly brand Muslims as foreigners, the mosques of Dreux fill up. Although many immigrants of Muslim background have ceased to practice their religion collectively, they return to a place of worship in the hope of regaining some dignity or perhaps simply in search of a little human warmth.

Dreux is in France. Its evolution and transformations may even seem particularly French when situated in the long historical process that scholars have been given the rather desperate job of explaining. Their mission—to recount the origins of the nation, to give grounding to its myths, to reconstruct its identity—may seem all the more desperate today, when the world is changing so quickly. It is no accident that Fernand Braudel's three-volume history of France carries the title *The Identity of France*.[24] This regrettably unfinished testament by one of the century's great French historians symbolizes an entire era of research. "Identity" has become a central issue of contemporary debate in France. It has found an echo elsewhere in Europe, where the concepts of nation and nationality are creating instability where once there was immobility. Yet no one has a very clear idea of what a nation's collective identity is, especially since the right has invoked the idea for the purpose of exclusion and intellectuals of the left have ventured onto the right's terrain in order to debate the issue of French identity.[25] It is useful to recall the words of Claude Lévi-Strauss, for whom identity is "like a focal point to which we inevitably must refer in order to explain certain things, though it never has a real existence."[26] Identity is therefore like a Russian nesting doll. It is carved wherever one lives, meaning first of all on one's home ground. The identity of belonging to the French nation fits inside of the identity that each of us forges around a certain plot of land, village, or neighborhood. We speak French with certain local accents and peculiarities of diction and syntax, and these distinctive features of language have nothing to do with where our parents were born. As anyone who has attended a national meeting of *beurs* (second-generation immigrants of Arab descent) can attest, it is striking to observe how each speaker can be identified immediately as coming from Marseilles, Belfort, or Lille even if their place of birth is never mentioned.

Along with millions of other French schoolchildren, I studied the standard textbook on medieval history in the "Petit Lavisse" series: "Our ancestors the Gauls were brave," it taught me. "Our ancestors the Franks were brave. Our ancestors the French were brave." I encountered those Gauls and Franks in the streets of Dreux when I left school, in my imagination clothing those who passed the foot of the castle ramparts in breeches and tunics. In the narrow streets of old Dreux I could imagine the medieval town, whose inhabitants resembled those portrayed on the stained-glass windows of Saint-Pierre. The people of Dreux had always built their buildings and monuments along those streets. What could I think but that Dreux enjoyed an existence unto itself, that it was a living creature that changed over the ages and wrapped itself in new costumes as it grew while remaining fundamentally the same? Marcel Dessal, one of Mayor Viollette's assistants as well as a trained historian and the author of a thesis on Charles Delescluze (a Drouais who fought for the Republic from the June Days to the Paris Commune), once gave me the works of Jules Michelet. Responsible for what today is called culture, Dessal took care of the young readers he met in the municipal library over which he reigned. In Michelet I read, as an overwhelming revelation, that if "England is an Empire, Germany a country and a race, France is a person."[27] Transposing this organicist conception of the history of my country to my city, I decided that Dreux too, even more than France, was a person, a collective being that had been born one day and had grown and would continue to grow. That being had its own "identity," upon which time could bestow new forms and dimensions, but its personality was unalterable.

In 1821, when Victor Hugo walked from Paris to Dreux to catch a glimpse of Adèle Foucher, whose family had sent her away from her importunate suitor, he saw no signs of a town as he approached. Neither the steeples of Saint-Pierre nor the belltower can be seen from a distance. To anyone driving today on National Highway 12, the high towers at Les Chamards looming up out of the wheatfields of the Beauce signal Dreux's presence. In Victor Hugo's time the children of Dreux had names like Paul and Louise, Jules and Marceline. Today they are called Grégory and Aïcha, Sandrine and Nourredine.

During my last campaign, in 1988, a young man named Nourredine worked on my staff. One day I asked him where he came from. He was at a loss for an answer. I reformulated the question: "What nationality are you?" This drew a stinging reply: "I am Drouais. I was born at Les Chamards." Nourredine grew up in Dreux, as I did. He knew Victor Hugo's poem "Le Vallon de Cherisy" because he had gone to public school and studied, as I had, the poem that Adèle Foucher's lover had written in a small village just outside Dreux on his way to see the woman of his dreams. Nourredine died in an automobile accident in August 1989 on his way back from Morocco, where he had gone on vacation with other young people from Dreux. And I still regret having asked him about his origins. By the tone of his reply I knew that my question had been taken, without my intending it, as questioning his legitimacy.

The "person" Dreux was thirty years ago has changed. She (I shall take her to be female) has changed so quickly that erstwhile residents say they can no longer recognize her. Not all of them have read Michelet, but all share an implicit sense of irreversible change as well as intense frustration. When they read in the papers or hear on radio or television that Dreux has become a "problem city," their sentiments are reinforced: their city has been the victim of a singular fate, and so have they. Nothing in the pronouncements of politicians has enabled them to understand or assimilate that change, to begin to make it a part of their collective history.

The response of Michel Rocard's government to the results of the December 1989 elections in Dreux pointed up the gap between the reality and the national leaders' understanding of that reality. Their announcement of measures intended to help integrate immigrants into French society was already a decade behind the times. In Dreux as elsewhere in France, first-generation immigrants were economically integrated and culturally excluded. Their children are products of French society, of its schools and their failures, of its suburbs and their inhumanity. And the children are culturally integrated but economically excluded. To focus attention on the integration of immigrants was to refuse to consider, beyond the nationality and background of disadvantaged groups within the population, the disintegration of working-class society. It was to refuse to consider the pain of being uprooted from one culture and having to put down roots in another, as people emigrating to Europe must do. Last but not least, it was to ignore the disarray, despair, and at times anger of French men and women of the same social and economic status as the immigrants, who live in the same buildings and housing developments and who know full well that their North African and Turkish neighbors have already integrated their destinies with the destiny of France. The "immigrant question" tends to mask the social question and, even more, the question of the deep changes that French society has undergone. Humanist cant is in no sense an answer to society's needs. Antiracist speeches, however necessary and laudable they may be, do not constitute a policy.

The government cannot find an approach. Should it assume that the problems faced by people of foreign descent are social issues to be dealt with by enforcing civil-rights laws? Or are special policies needed, such as establishing quotas for the integration of victims of national or ethnic discrimination? Officials no longer know whether to extol France as the embodiment of universalist principles or to emphasize the enrichment made possible by the acknowledgment of difference. The fact that public speeches and official documents have begun to include expressions such as "foreign communities" and "communities of foreign origin" have oddly enough stirred no national debate, even though the term "community" challenges the constitutional principle that France is one and indivisible. Tacit acceptance of that principle has made it possible to secure national cohesion despite special regional interests, religious diversity, and class antagonisms.

People should have been astonished to hear representatives of the government—and especially of a left-wing government—pointing to the existence of distinct communities within the French nation. What and whom were they referring to? Do immigrants and their children constitute a community? Were officials who used the word thinking of certain immigrants whose relation to France is special, namely, those born in the former colonies of the empire and in what used to be French départements in Algeria? Should they include the citizens of France's overseas territories? These are serious questions. In attempting, for the sake of convenience, to "ethnicize" social issues and problems, politicians run the risk of creating lobbies. Lobbies turn communities that often are more mythical than real into the stock-in-trade of those elusive groups' self-proclaimed leaders. Taking this path encourages "differentialist discourse" and can give rise to a xenophobic ideology that benefits the extreme right. France has never been "one." But by proclaiming itself one nation, it did become indivisible. At a time when the nations of Europe are on a planned march toward integration, it may be useful to weigh the threat to unity that recognizing ethnic and national communities may entail.

History will no doubt accuse France's rulers of myopia. It may also note that the greatest thinkers of the day did not always properly appreciate the consequences of population movements from the southern to the northern hemisphere. Even Fernand Braudel, who defined the identity of France as an amalgam of additions and comminglings, referred to foreigners as "them" and to the French as "us."[28] Not to accept the fact that in Dreux "we" and "they" form a single whole that constitutes the city of tomorrow is to hide our heads in the sand. Such a refusal to look facts in the face is a problem not only for one tiny subprefecture at the juncture of the Beauce, Ile-de-France, and Normandy but for France as a whole.

To quote Braudel once again: "Every national identity necessarily implies a certain national unity. It is, in a sense, the reflection, the transposition, the condition of that unity."[29] Since the time of Ernest Renan (1823–1892), many people in France have agreed with his view that a nation is "a clearly expressed desire to continue life in common."[30] That life in common unfolds, inexorably and not without difficulty, in France's cities and villages. It has always involved additions and comminglings, but these never impaired the national unity given the requisite desire, will, and shared values.

In Search of a Common Denominator

The longer one ponders Dreux, the more difficult it becomes to detect any "collective identity" in this heterogeneous urban ensemble. The territorial unity that gave the city its name has given way to bewildering diversity and scattering. It is difficult to make out anything other than a multiplicity of divergent views in the mosaic of memories and histories that coexist in Dreux. There is not one dominant culture in the city but many cultures superimposed and often at odds. Nothing is new in this: the idea that identity is the product of a homogeneous and stable population smacks of myth. But the demographic upheaval and atomization of the city appear to have accentuated distinctions and sharpened differences. How, then, does one define Dreux?

It is tempting to make a first stab at a definition by giving one consistent with available statistics: Dreux is a working-class city. It is true that the majority of the population consists of blue-collar workers, both skilled and unskilled. This approach is ultimately unsatisfying, however, because while Dreux is a city of workers, what is called the working class is fragmented and has no shared "consciousness." There are French workers and foreign workers, foreigners and immigrants who have become French, tenants and aspiring propertyowners, people with steady jobs and people on temporary contract, the unemployed and the employed. Sociologists like to classify, but behind the criterion of socioeconomic status lurk a hundred subtle differences that are a source of division and sometimes conflict.

Is there space for communication in the city? In Dreux communication for the most part takes the form of chronic rumors, which are often sources of anxiety and even terror. At the core of the city's political, organizational, religious, and cultural life is a group of no more than five hundred people. Within this core group, people and information do circulate, but there is little input from outside. The local microculture is in fact the culture of this group of citizens of the valley, and little of it filters out to the rest of the city. At inaugurations, openings, and lectures the same people gather time after time. Trade unions are weak. Tenant associations are all but nonexistent. Parent-teacher organizations are kept going by a small number of active members. Athletic clubs and singles clubs do serve a relatively large number of people, but despite the efforts of a few volunteers these are mainly for-profit businesses rather than democratic meeting places for people sharing similar concerns and objectives.

Does the expression of political views foster a sense of civic belonging? Leaving times of national crisis aside, the only real opportunity to gauge a city's "state of mind" occurs when its citizens come together to choose their representatives. If we look at Dreux once more in light of the political changes that have taken place there, one question is inescapable. Can the National Front, operating on the ruins of a crumbling society and taking advantage of the errors and misjudgments of its democratic opponents, offer the citizens of Dreux a common denominator for reconstructing a mythical identity?

The Irresistible Rise of the Right

• 3 •

In describing the history of Dreux from the turn of the century to 1965, people usually say that the city was a Radical bastion, a paragon of political stability. True enough, from 1908 to 1958 Dreux elected the same mayor, Maurice Viollette, over and over again. But Viollette, despite the assertions of several historians, never belonged to the Radical Party. He was too independent to accept socialist discipline and too socialist to identify with the more moderate Radicals. As a deputy in Paris early in the century, he was an independent socialist; later he joined the Socialist Republican Party, more a loose association of deputies than a political party in the ordinary sense. After the Liberation he joined François Mitterrand's UDSR (Union Démocratique et Socialiste de la Résistance). In the Eure-et-Loir, where these small groups had no presence other than Viollette himself, he was simply "a republican." Dreux voters accepted his independence. At each new election a majority of them supported his slate, rallying behind this illustrious local politician who over the course of the century had acquired national stature. It would be misleading, however, to suggest that at home Viollette hid his true colors. In 1919 he chose to run on a resolutely left-wing slate and lose the election rather than lend his support to the Union Nationale, which promoted what he considered an intolerable blurring of party lines. In

1924 he ardently supported the Cartel des Gauches. In 1936 he did not hide his enthusiasm for the Popular Front and ultimately served as a minister in a Popular Front government.

Viollette's weekly newspaper, *L'Action républicaine,* was his forum, and his editorials reflect a vigorously independent mind formed in the days of Boulangism and the Dreyfus Affair.[1] For Viollette, the Republic had enemies on the right who dreamed of undoing the accomplishments of the revolution, and supporters on the left who became adversaries when they refused to join in a common front against the omnipresent threat of reaction. Over the years Viollette created a network of loyal supporters in Dreux, groups ranging from the powerful and combative Cercle Laïque and the local Freemasons to the Union Commerciale, which together controlled the city.

The right, long represented by the Christian Democrats, themselves the heirs of Orleanists who ultimately accepted the Republic, strove to fill the role of loyal opposition but was reduced to that of witness. In the interwar period there had been a few local members of the extreme-right Croix de Feu, and the emergence of a very active local branch of the RPF (Rassemblement du Peuple Français) in 1947 surprised no one. But the extreme right, support for which was limited to a few families in central Dreux, had no power in the voting booth. In 1956 the Poujadists staged some impressive demonstrations when the tax collectors arrived in town to inspect the inventories of local tradespeople, but they fared less well at the polls in Dreux than in the surrounding rural cantons. The bourgeois right, with its Vichyite or Bonapartist roots, never joined forces with the angry merchants who supported the Poujadists.

In short, Dreux was a model of stability for two-thirds of a century. Nothing in the history of this quiet, moderate little town suggested that it would become the birthplace of extremism.

The Turbulence

It was in 1965 that Dreux, unnoticed at the time, embarked on an era of instability and turbulence. In 1959 Maurice Viollette, then eighty-nine years old, ran for municipal office for the last time. He was number two on the slate, having decided, to no one's surprise, to give up the first spot. Georges Rastel, a high-ranking civil servant and former prefect of the département, was Viollette's hand-picked successor; the former mayor did not feel that any of the members of his city-hall staff were worthy of succeeding him. Six years later, Rastel was badly beaten by a right-wing slate headed by the MRP (Mouvement Républicain Populaire).

Had the city changed politically as a result of an influx of new residents? The fact that the area had become more working-class might suggest that the left—the socialist and communist parties—should have reaped the benefits of the changes. And that was what happened in the first round of the March 1965 municipal elections. The two left-wing slates (the Radical on the one hand and the Socialist-Communist on the other, Socialists and Communists having agreed to run a joint slate even though they would not formally unite under the aegis of the Common Program until 1977) garnered the vast majority of the votes: 62 percent. But Rastel was not sure which party he wanted to ally with in the second round, and the consequences of this indecision were unexpected. After much shilly-shallying, he finally merged his Radical slate with the Socialist-Communist slate. The Communists, irritated by Rastel's behavior and buoyed by their strong showing in the first round, passed the word to their supporters to vote for the combined left-wing slate but only after crossing out Rastel's name. Many voters were dismayed by this backstabbing and tactical maneuvering and in any case were of mixed minds about the mayor, who was not only an "outsider" but also different, sociologically speaking, from his electorate; some chose to vote for the right-wing ticket. The right, much to its surprise, won the election. For the leaders of the left, which had held the city since the turn of the century and never imagined that Dreux could slip from its grasp, it was a rude awakening. The "republican" electorate, disturbed by the personal rivalries and struggles of their leaders (which would continue in the future) and feeling betrayed by their representatives, had reasserted their independence.

It is worth looking beyond these immediate factors to more remote causes of the sudden change in Dreux's political complexion in 1965. The left had of course always seen itself as the "party of the republic," but what exactly did that mean after the advent of the Fifth Republic under Charles de Gaulle? De Gaulle's assumption of power created a new situation in Dreux and elsewhere. In May 1958 Maurice Viollette, that exemplary figure of the Third Republic, whose editorials had repeatedly condemned General de Gaulle as a latter-day Boulanger, denounced the "coup d'état." Going back even farther in French history, he compared de Gaulle's return to the coup d'état of Louis Napoleon, the specter that had haunted his republican youth: "Woe and misery! Our poor country is dying. The man who once could pride himself on having saved it now wants to kill it. It is *L'Histoire d'un crime* all over again. The comparison is striking: 'the African generals' are indicted on every page of Hugo's remarkable work. Today's African generals are repeating the history of the previous century. The General Salan of that earlier time was named Saint-Arnaud. What is more, the coup d'état, now as then, is clerical as well as military. In 1851 Bishop Sibour celebrated a mass of thanksgiving in honor of the coup. And this past Sunday, in Colombey, a papal high mass was celebrated for de Gaulle, on the very anniversary of the crime of Ajaccio."[2]

In September, however, Viollette joined the Gaullists, though he continued to express himself in the idiom of the Third Republic. He had been mistaken, he conceded. De Gaulle was not a seditious conspirator. The proof was that he had chosen 4 September—the anniversary of the birth of the Third Republic—to proclaim the new constitution and had chosen to do it on the Place de la République. Of course the new constitution was by no means perfect. To Viollette's way of thinking, its Caesarist characteristics were shocking, but the republican symbols that presided over its birth were of some comfort. De Gaulle, Viollette reasoned, would emulate Galliffet: General Gaston de Galliffet, the minister of Waldeck-Rousseau, the republican who had forced the army to accept the discipline of the Republic. Viollette was by now convinced that de Gaulle would do the same. He urged his readers to vote yes on the referendum. Dreux voters approved the constitution by a majority of 81 percent, slightly higher than the national average.

The election of Jean Cauchon as mayor in 1965 came about at a time when ancient rivalries were on the wane. Although memory of old quarrels had not yet been entirely effaced, the decision by Radicals in Dreux—and more generally throughout the Beauce—to throw their support to the Gaullists created an entirely new situation. How did things stand now? Clear-headed anti-Gaullists found it even more difficult to read the new situation in light of the results of the referendum on the Fifth Republic and the subsequent legislative elections: if the left identified with the opposition to de Gaulle and his ticket, it stood to lose the support of more than just Radicals. Some Communists and Socialists had also voted for the Gaullists. The municipal election of 1965 demonstrated the depths of the confusion. In the second round the left was ostensibly united. In fact, however, it was deeply divided and did itself in, as we have seen. The Communist Party surreptitiously worked for the defeat of the unified left-wing ticket in order to oust the pro-Gaullist Radical mayor. A young man, previously unknown in political circles, spoke at the traditional public meeting on the eve of the voting and delivered a devastating attack on the incumbent mayor, thereby openly aiding the right-wing slate. (That young man was Georges Lemoine, and twelve years later he would be elected mayor of Chartres on a Socialist ticket.) On the day after the elections, the Dreux left discovered that, more than simply losing an election, it had in fact been demolished. The Viollettists consoled themselves by organizing an annual commemoration of the great man's achievements. The Socialists, divided between the SFIO (Section Française de l'Internationale Ouvrière) and the PSA (Parti Socialiste Autonome), were a small force without a leader.

In 1971 Jean Cauchon was triumphantly reelected, capturing

68 percent of the vote against a unified left-wing slate led by a member of the MRG (Mouvement des Radicaux de Gauche). But then in 1977, after a total of twelve years in office, he was roundly defeated. This time the victorious left-wing slate was led by the Socialist Party, which had made steady progress in every election since the 1971 party congress at Epinay and finally, for the first time in the history of Dreux, outpolled both the Radicals and the Communists. And so it was that I became mayor. In the spring of 1977 party leader François Mitterrand came to Dreux to hail the arrival of a new generation of socialists in city government. Dreux was seen as exemplifying the renaissance of a united left resolutely on the march toward victory in the upcoming parliamentary elections.

Six years later, Dreux was once again the focus of attention. To observers of French politics and professional commentators, it was in Dreux that the National Front was born as a political force. More precisely, it was born on Sunday, 4 September 1983. On that day a slate headed by the secretary-general of the National Front captured 17 percent of the votes cast in a municipal by-election.

Earlier, in March 1983, the Front had sponsored slates of candidates in elections held in seven of Paris' twenty arrondissements (wards) as well as in Nice, Montpellier, and Clermont-Ferrand. The Front's participation had complicated the electoral picture, adding some nastiness to the debate, and its vote totals could not be dismissed as negligible: the party's leader, Jean-Marie Le Pen, had himself been elected city councillor for Paris' twentieth arrondissement. In some places, such as Marseilles, slates that made no mention of any affiliation with the National Front ran on a xenophobic, anticrime platform, traditionally the province of the extreme right. In other cities National Front candidates, with the connivence of the conservative RPR, discreetly appeared on that party's ticket, hiding their true colors. This happened not only in Dreux but in Grasse, Antibes, and Le Cannet, three communes in the Alpes-Maritimes, as well as in Isère, Indre-et-Loire, and the

Paris region. No one at the time was particularly upset by these successes, which were modest and isolated, or by the alliances between the Front and the RPR, which were limited in scope and not publicly announced.

It was the September 1983 elections in Dreux that broke the mold in spectacular fashion, suggesting some astonishing form of spontaneous generation. This idea cannot withstand scrutiny, however: Marie-France Stirbois was accurate when she said, six years later, that she "had not fallen from the sky into the seat of deputy."[3] Her success was the result of patient groundwork that had escaped political commentators. The twelve years between Jean-Pierre Stirbois's initial 1977 candidacy and Marie-France Stirbois's 1989 election as deputy are of more than local interest. The history of that period reflects something going on all across France.

The National Front Makes Its Debut

Voters in the Eure-et-Loir's second district exhibited no reaction to the announcement, on the first Sunday of February 1978, that the unknown Jean-Pierre Stirbois would be a candidate for the National Assembly in the March elections. The announcement was treated as a nonevent; marginal candidates run in every election. This particular candidate was running under the aegis of the National Front, a small extremist party headed by Jean-Marie Le Pen, who had served briefly as a Poujadist deputy and was an outspoken proponent of a French Algeria. The National Front was born in 1972 as a federation of various splinter parties, the remnants of an anti-Gaullist right with nostalgic longings for the wartime politics of Marshal Pétain.

Stirbois did not announce his candidacy in the usual way, which in the provinces means either calling a press conference or issuing a communiqué addressed to the local newspapers. Instead journalists learned of his decision just as everyone else did: they found the candidate's eight-page tract, in which he introduced himself and his program, under the windshield wipers of their automobiles.

Stirbois, aged thirty-three, married, father of two, and manager of a business with eight employees, described himself as an "ordinary voter from the Dreux area." Few people in Dreux were aware, however, that this ordinary voter was not actually a resident of the city but a visitor who occasionally spent weekends on his parents-in-law's property in Ecluzelles, a small nearby village. No one was interested in his biography. Even if people did know that the candidate had been involved in several investigations and various scrapes with the law since 1967, they could not have discussed these facts in public because the amnesty of 1974 had stricken them from the official record. Stirbois was a street activist, a former member of such extreme-right-wing groups as the Comités Tixier-Vignancour, the Mouvement Jeune Révolution, the Mouvement Solidariste Français (affiliated with Pierre Sergent's OAS–Metro), and the Groupe Action Jeunesse. He and some of his Solidarist friends had only recently joined the National Front, intending to shift their activities from the streets to the political arena. Henceforth their weapon of preference would be the ballot box rather than the billy club.

Neither Martial Taugourdeau, a country doctor who was the RPR's candidate for deputy, nor Maurice Legendre, a beekeeper who was the Socialist incumbent—both men with solid roots in the Dreux region—paid any attention to the new candidate. They had no idea that Stirbois's wife was also a candidate in the legislative elections: she ran for the position of adjunct deputy *(suppléante)* in Seine-Saint-Denis, Georges Marchais's district. In Dreux, Taugourdeau and Legendre knew that they would face each other in the second round of the legislative elections. Since 1958 the seat had been held either by a Gaullist or a Socialist.

This was the first legislative campaign in which Taugourdeau, a *conseiller général* and mayor of a rural commune, headed the ticket. His goal was to reclaim for the right a seat once held by Edmond Thorailler, a leading figure of the RPR and long-time conservative, who had been elected deputy in 1958 only to fall to a Socialist in 1967 before winning again in 1968 and then going down to defeat one last time in 1973. Taugourdeau's task was not easy, however: Thorailler, the amiable notary, mayor of an important town in the region, and leading light among local Gaullists, had for the past several months been in jail for fraud.

Stirbois's limited campaign lent credence to the idea that he had run only to make his party's existence known. The candidate held a press conference in Chartres, assisted by his "press secretary," Michel Collinot, who was himself a candidate for deputy in Seine-Saint-Denis on the same ticket with Stirbois's wife. The only issues that came up were immigration and crime. Stirbois stated that his goal was to make sure that neither the right nor the left would emerge with a majority in the Dreux district. In subsequent days he did not make the traditional round of the district's communes. His press secretary appears not to have been unduly burdened with work: a brief communiqué was issued on 15 February. It dealt mainly with the threat of immigration in Dreux and revealed that the candidate's slogan was "French first!"

In early March a local newspaper, *La République du centre*, published an article on Stirbois by a reporter who had covered the candidate's appearance at Dreux's Sunday market. The market was located on the city's southern heights, where a high percentage of the population is of North African descent. Political activists of the left and extreme left like to work the crowds at this colorful, festive event. A newspaper article about Stirbois's appearance featured a photograph of a group of individuals with an obvious fondness for military attire. Among them was a woman, Marie-France Stirbois, who was shown distributing brochures along with her comrades. The caption reads: "Combat boots, battle fatigues, and balaclava helmets, these are M. Stirbois's G-Men . . . obviously determined to wage a muscular campaign." As for the campaign's tactics, the journalist had this to say: "There was one tense moment last Sunday, though, when a group of militants of the extreme left observed a landing by militants of the extreme right backing M. Stirbois of the National Front. To the leftists the sight of paratroop boots and combat fatigues was like the sight of a red cape to a bull, a reaction not mitigated by the fact that the rightists, without authorization, had just plastered the area with posters whose text was crisp and to the point: 'Leftists! Don't trouble your heads—we'll smash your skulls instead!' "[4] Stirbois responded to the article with mockery: "My supporters wearing boots and helmets? It was cold . . . Should our people have to go barefoot?"

Clearly the press did not take the National Front candidate seriously. Local journalists drew a parallel between the extreme left and the extreme right and portrayed the one as the natural enemy of the other. As far as the established political parties were concerned, Stirbois's only function was to represent the outmoded ideas of the past. He and they were not playing in the same ballgame. When a small group of National Front militants seized a shipment of one regional paper that had refused to publish its candidate's statement, everyone said that the incident was regrettable but insignificant.

In the first round of voting, Stirbois garnered 2 percent of the vote in the district overall as well as in the city of Dreux proper. Who were the 252 Dreux voters who cast their ballots for the National Front candidate? Were they people nostalgic for Vichy? There must have been a few of those in central Dreux, where few local merchants had distinguished themselves in the Resistance prior to D-Day. Or were they veterans of France's wars in Indochina and Algeria with whom decolonization did not sit well? The OAS had a small but active group in the city. But such sentiments remained in the background.[5]

At this stage, the outcome of the second round appeared uncertain. Two extreme-left candidates and the Communist candidate (who had received more than 15 percent of the votes cast in the first round) agreed to stand aside in favor of the Socialist. Despite a strong challenge by the candidate of the CDS (Centre des Démocrates Sociaux), Taugourdeau emerged as the leading vote-getter on the right. In a sense, Jean-Pierre Stirbois had made good on his wager. His modest 2 percent represented a problem for the right, which mathematically needed those votes to win. But there was also another question: what would become of the 2.8 percent of the first-round vote that had gone to the Parti Social Démocrate? This was a rather strange affair: the party's candidate was a former colonel who had trained his fire mainly on the CDS candidate. Was this coincidental, or had the whole campaign been orchestrated by parties unknown? The question can legitimately be raised because it has been proven that, in a subsequent cantonal election, the National Front secretly promoted a candidate in order to take votes away from the candidate of the moderate right. It is not inconceivable that Stirbois, in his first Dreux campaign, resorted to the same strategy. If—a clever tactician may have reasoned—the conservative vote could be whittled away on both its right and its left extremes, the traditional right might emerge from the first round in the minority and therefore be forced to enter into an alliance with the extreme right. The unknown Stirbois may well have tested his mettle as a tactician in this Dreux election. Ten years later his tactical skills would help to destabilize the right, which in election after election was forced to confront the burning issue of its relations with Jean-Marie Le Pen.

Did Martial Taugourdeau meet with the National Front candidate after the first round of the 1978 legislative elections? No one has ever said so publicly. Was Stirbois tempted to strike a bargain with the RPR candidate over the 1,332 votes he had won in the district? No evidence of such a bargain exists. If there were negotiations, they evidently failed: the National Front did not call on its voters to support the RPR candidate in the second round. Nevertheless, Taugourdeau won with 51.2 percent of the vote, recapturing the seat for the right. He was the favorite of rural voters. The city of Dreux itself gave the left-wing candidate a comfortable majority of 52.5 percent.

Hard-Hitting Slogans and Confrontations

Cantonal elections, in which the members of the Conseil Général (the departmental governing body) are chosen, are of interest primarily to the local elite. They rarely arouse much passion, except perhaps in rural precincts. When city people have a problem, they take it to the mayor. Most voters have no clear idea of what a *conseiller général* does. Indeed, the role would be clearer if the post were referred to as *conseiller départemental*. Some people even think that the *conseillers généraux* are elected by the *conseillers municipaux*, or members of the city council.

The canton known as Dreux Southwest—of two Dreux cantons the only one to hold elections in March 1979—comprises a good half of Dreux (including the working-class neighborhoods of the southern heights) along with two suburban communes (Vernouillet and Luray) and ten rural communes. There was no great rush on the right to replace the retiring incumbent, Maurice Legendre, the mayor of Vernouillet and a former Socialist deputy who had served as *conseiller général* since 1967 and was reelected in 1973 by a majority of almost 60 percent. Nor was there any great contention on the left to succeed Legendre. Elections of this kind rarely arouse the interest of the extreme left, whose revolutionary rhetoric is ill equipped to deal with such mundane matters as school busing and drainage systems, the staple of politics at this level.

But Jean-Pierre Stirbois did choose to run. For the first time, National Front posters appeared on the walls of Dreux: "One million unemployed, one million immigrants too many. French first!" The candidate of the extreme right also began making appearances in the working-class neighborhoods of Dreux. As in his previous legislative campaign, he confined his speeches to immigration and crime. But now these themes were systematically tailored to appeal to a group of voters much larger than the fringe of Pétainist and pro-colonial veterans, who were solidly behind Stirbois anyway. The new group he was aiming at consisted of those who had voted Communist in the past. In a press release of 7 March, for example, Stirbois charged that "the CGT [Confédération Générale du Travail, the Communist-dominated union] is betraying French workers." The text went on to say that by defending foreign workers, the CGT and the Communist Party were conspiring against the French working class. The next day, local and regional papers published a second press release issued by a group that did not really exist, the so-called Eure-et-Loir Federation of the National Front, denouncing the growing number of immigrants in the Dreux area and demanding that police be assigned to keep the peace at local dances, which it said were being disrupted by gangs of juvenile delinquents, with the implication that these juveniles were immigrants.

Yet Stirbois's candidacy attracted little attention until it was announced that Jean-Marie Le Pen himself would appear locally in support of his party's candidate. This stirred the passions of the extreme left and thrust Stirbois's name into the limelight. A hall was reserved in Dreux for the Front's final campaign rally, at which Le Pen was scheduled to be the featured speaker.

In March 1979 the leader of the National Front was still a minor figure on the national political scene. Nevertheless, soon after his appearance was announced, the press published a number of announcements of counterdemonstrations by extreme-left and human-rights groups. As mayor, I received a number of petitions. Delegations from various groups came to warn me that they too intended to protest. After notifying the prefect, I issued an order banning the proposed meeting as a threat to law and order. The National Front then applied to the town of Vernouillet for a permit, but the town council refused to allow the use of its meeting hall. Instead it made the symbolic gesture of reserving the hall for a dance sponsored by an antiracist organization on the night Le Pen was scheduled to appear.

On 14 March the Socialist candidate for the cantonal post held his final public rally in the small town of Luray. At 9 o'clock that evening, some thirty spectators, mostly retirees living in the town, turned up at the local meeting hall. The police, having received word that extreme-right-wing militants from Paris planned to disrupt the meeting, informed Socialist Party officials that since the proposed rally was public, they couldn't prevent anyone from entering. They would, however, patrol the access roads to the village and station policemen outside the hall. Anyone not from the local area who looked suspicious or threatening would be subjected to a legal search, and any weapons or dangerous instruments found in their possession would be confiscated.

The meeting began as scheduled. The people in the audience had already made up their minds about how to vote and sat quietly in their chairs. The speakers sat behind a long table, while the meeting was chaired by the Communist mayor. My turn came to speak. I had begun explaining why the budget of the Conseil Général was important to the daily lives of citizens when a group of twenty youths with crew cuts and wearing long raincoats began to filter into the hall one by one; their entry was slowed by the police search at the door. They were not from the area, except one whose extremist views were well known. All kept their hands in their pockets. Noticing this, a few Socialist activists went and sat down behind the new arrivals to keep an eye on what they were up to. Among those who entered the hall was Jean-Pierre Stirbois.

When the time came for comments from the floor, Stirbois rose from his chair. He too kept his hands in the pockets of a raincoat held closed by a belt with a large buckle. A short, brown-haired man, he thrust his chin out and addressed some heated words toward the podium. In the name of democracy he called on me to pledge then and there that I would authorize a future appearance in Dreux by Jean-Marie Le Pen. When I answered that as long as I was mayor and a Le Pen appearance posed a threat to law and order, I would remain opposed. I expected a riposte from Stirbois. Instead he and his companions withdrew their hands from their pockets and began hurling eggs at the podium. The police stationed out front had rightly judged that projectiles of this type were not dangerous instruments.

Meanwhile, the antiracist group held its dance in Vernouillet. Others, believing that it was better to talk than to dance, held a meeting at a place of historical importance in the history of the local left, the Cercle Laïque of Dreux, where they protested against the ideas of the National Front. Their protest was symbolic—and feeble. There was a good deal of overlap between antiracist and extreme-left groups anyway: all drew on the same handful of active militants who wished, in a messianic spirit, to bring their gospel to the working class. Their enthusiasm drew the attention of the local press, which published their communiqués, but their ideological rhetoric had only the narrowest of audiences. On this particular night, they proved that antiracism could mobilize no one but themselves, and even then the various factions could not agree on how best to proceed: some wanted to dance, others to talk. How many people, in any case, had turned out for all three events—the dance, the debate, and the public rally? A mere two hundred at most. In Dreux that night, most people were either asleep or watching television, unconcerned by either racism or antiracism.

In the cantonal elections, the National Front gave proof that it had indeed found an audience. Although the Socialist candidate was elected in the first round, the left in six years had lost 10 percent of its vote, and slightly more than 7 of that 10-percent loss was incurred by the Socialist Party alone. Stirbois received 8.5 percent of the votes cast. In Dreux 303 people voted for him.

Stirbois was not pressed by the authorities for disrupting the rally in Luray. He was questioned by the Paris police the following June, however. Backed by a group of extremist youths (some of whom may have been with him in Dreux in March), he had attempted to shout down Simone Veil at a rally prior to the European parliamentary elections. The disruptive group shouted insults at the former minister of health, whom they called an abortionist (alluding to her sponsorship of legalized abortion), on top of which they added some choice antisemitic abuse. As a result, the secretary-general of the National Front wound up spending several hours at police headquarters in the eighteenth arrondissement.

The Socialist Tide Rolls In

After being elected president of France on 10 May 1981, François Mitterrand announced that he was dissolving the National Assembly. Postelection ceremonies at the Pantheon kicked off the campaign for new legislative elections.

Jean-Pierre Stirbois was a candidate for the seat of deputy from Dreux. So was I. Both of us were challenging the RPR incumbent. After the first round, the combined left vote (including the extreme left) was 50.5 percent, while the traditional right garnered 47.3 percent. Stirbois, with the remaining 2.2 percent, held the key to victory in the second round, which promised to be close. Still, the National Front had suffered a sharp setback since the cantonal elections. Yet even if it had fallen back to its 1978 level, the party was not without influence. The RPR candidate needed that 2.2 percent if he wanted to hold on to his seat.

Two nights before the voting, I met my RPR opponent in a public debate. Afterwards I asked him if Stirbois had contacted him. Yes, the National Front candidate had asked for a million francs, he said, in exchange for withdrawing from the race. "I would rather lose," my opponent said, "than make such a deal. It has nothing to do with money. It's a question of principle."

In the first round, the Socialist Party by itself received 40.63 percent of the vote in the district and 44.1 percent in Dreux. As in the rest of France, the Socialist tide had rolled in. In the second round, I was elected deputy with 51.4 percent of the vote.

The Socialist vote in Dreux, where I won with 55.7 percent, was better even than in the municipal elections of March 1977. The Communist vote had dropped from 15 to 9 percent in the district between 1978 and 1981, and there was talk about party collapse. The right, after such a devastating defeat, was in disarray. Only a few conservative diehards remained in the hall on the night of the elections long enough to hear the final results. Most of the right-wing crowd, including local party leaders, went home early: the sky had fallen. One industrialist, known for his outspokenness, was heard to say that the time had come to get out of France. With Mitterrand in the Elysée, Communists in the government, and a left-wing majority in the parliament, revolution seemed just around the corner.

A Mysterious Letter

Half the seats on the Conseil Général come up for reelection every three years, and in March 1982 it was time for another cantonal election. Since the last election, cantonal boundaries had been redrawn to take account of population shifts. Dreux now comprised three cantons rather than two. In this election, two of these three seats were up for grabs. Based on the results of the previous election, one seemed winnable for the left, while the other seemed likely to stay with the right. Both Jean-Pierre Stirbois and his wife Marie-France Stirbois were candidates.

Less than a year after Mitterrand's election to the presidency and the Socialist Party's capture of an absolute majority in parliament, the political climate had turned against the left. The "state of grace," as Mitterrand's honeymoon period was dubbed by the French press, was long since over. What had revived the opposition was none other than the immigrant question, and in particular the foreign minister's mention, during a visit to Algiers, of the possibility of granting foreigners the right to vote in municipal elections. Meanwhile, tensions in Dreux were growing. Copies of a letter allegedly written by an Algerian living in France to a friend back home had been circulating since the summer of 1981. The text read in part: "Dear Mustapha. By the grace of all-powerful Allah we have become the lords and masters of Paris. I wonder why you hesitate to join us." Mustapha's friend goes on to enumerate all the benefits that France holds in store for him, his children, and his women and then closes with a flourish: "So you see that your presence here is indispensable, and who knows if you might not be elected to the future council of émigrés. Come soon. Lots of us await your arrival, because Mitterrand has promised to grant us the right to vote very soon now. We kicked the French out of Algeria. Why shouldn't we do the same thing here?"

The owner of a fashionable bistro in the center of town, an

ex-member of the Parti Socialiste Unifié, was the first person to show me this document. To him it was a good joke, a prank and not so far wrong in its contents. He also said he had passed it on to numerous acquaintances. This was in late July 1981.

Starting with this campaign, Dreux would serve as a testing site for various forms of racist, anti-Arab propaganda. The tests were appalling but effective. Eighteen months later, this same letter would be circulated throughout France during the 1983 legislative election campaign. It became so well known, in fact, that Patrick Jarreau wrote an article printed on the front page of *Le Monde* under the title "Dear Mustapha." It was only then that people realized how widely the letter had circulated. New tracts appeared claiming that "the immigrants are always right." Variations on the Mustapha letter also appeared: in one, Mustapha is the cousin rather than the friend of the writer, and he is urged to come to France to "pluck the pullets clean." When a pamphlet containing one such purported letter was posted on the bulletin board of a small company outside Paris, an immigrant worker went to the plant manager to protest, only to be told that "it's just a political flyer."

Who initiated the Mustapha letter? Nobody knows. It appears to have surfaced first in Dreux, which, given the composition of its population and the presence of the xenophobic virus, was an ideal proving ground. At the time, the extreme right had no headquarters in the city and only two or three known activists. The National Front's office was no more than a mail drop, actually a post-office box rented by a plant manager who led a quiet life out of the public eye. Given his past, it is easy to understand why he shunned publicity: he had been a participant in Vichy's Chantiers de Jeunesse (Youth Works Projects) and had served as a group leader in charge of training recruits to the Militia *(la Milice)*, the paramilitary collaborationist organization that provided the Vichy regime's muscle. After the Liberation he fled, probably to Spain. Resistance fighters from the Lot-et-Garonne who survived the Militia's punitive searches and strong-arm interrogations still remember him. He was sentenced, in absentia, to death for treason, armed combat against France, and intelligence with the enemy. In

1952, after French war criminals were amnestied, he surfaced and was arrested for flight to avoid prosecution in 1945. In 1953 he was sentenced to five years at hard labor.[6] A few months later the sentence was suspended.

This man seems to have been Jean-Pierre Stirbois's only operative in Dreux in 1981. Stirbois himself lived in the Paris suburb of Neuilly and occasionally visited his parents-in-law at Ecluzelles. During those visits he probably met with local sympathizers at the home of the former Militia officer. Who were they? In a small town, people know who is friendly with whom. Among the friends of the former officer—no one in Dreux knew anything about his past—were several prominent local figures, including a doctor who had been the local contact of the OAS.

After the voting in the cantonal elections of 18 March 1982, the former Militia officer and his friends, several of whom had spent time hiding out or in prison after the war, must have experienced the sweet joy of revenge. After a campaign that had involved neither shock tactics nor violence, the National Front received a higher percentage of the vote than any extreme-right-wing group had obtained since Poujadism in the 1950s. In the canton where Jean-Pierre Stirbois was the candidate, the party captured 12.6 percent of the vote, while in the other canton, where his wife was making her political debut, it won 9.5 percent.

In the campaign the two Stirbois appealed to different groups. He courted the working-class vote by once again denouncing the Communist Party's alleged collusion with immigrants against the interests of French workers, while she issued position papers denouncing the so-called *taxe professionnelle* in a move designed to attract the votes of merchants and professionals. She also issued a warning against the "Marxization of teaching" in the public schools in an appeal for the family vote. Last but not least, both cantons were flooded with brochures blaming the invasion of France by "hordes of immigrants" on the parties of both the right and the left.

In the second round of voting, Michel Lethuillier, who had left a small independent party (the CNIP) for the RPR, was able to win without the votes that the National Front had claimed in the first round. But Jean-René Fontanille, the RPR candidate in the other canton, needed those votes. Were there negotiations between the RPR and the National Front after the first round? The city was rife with rumors concerning the alleged details of a bargain between the two parties. Only one thing can be said for sure: the National Front, which in previous elections had never advised its supporters how to vote in the second round, this time issued a statement to the press. Jean-Pierre and Marie-France Stirbois thanked the people who had voted for them in the first round and urged them to vote in the second round for the "candidates of the united opposition." This was the first mention of any union involving the National Front. The two Stirbois then withdrew in favor of Fontanille and Lethuillier. What is more, the Stirbois press release was printed up in pamphlet form and distributed house to house. Already Jean-Pierre Stirbois was laying the groundwork for the future. On 22 March 1982 he wrote that "it is important that the battle of the upcoming municipal elections be waged by a united opposition."

Fontanille and Lethuillier were both elected in the second round. In a book published in 1988, Stirbois alludes to his negotiations with the RPR between the two rounds of voting, but gives no details other than to say that Fontanille, the top RPR official in the département, agreed to accept his endorsement. In return, the National Front was to be included in the united opposition slate in the upcoming municipal elections. It was thus by way of the March 1982 cantonal elections that the National Front was able to work its way into the big leagues of French politics.

The Right and the Extreme Right Join Hands

A year earlier, the Dreux right found itself without a leader, unless perhaps it was Jean Cauchon, the former CDS mayor. After the March 1982 cantonal elections, it discovered a new leader in the freshly elected Jean-René Fontanille, a lawyer and former alternate deputy to Jacques Toubon in Paris. Who would head the right-wing slate of candidates opposing the incumbent left-wing city government?

By October 1982 the National Front was testing its influence within the local right. Jean-Pierre Stirbois held a press conference that revealed just how tense the ongoing negotiations were. In order to force the hand of the traditional right, Stirbois stated that he was prepared to run his own list of candidates: "We are the only party capable of taking votes from the left on issues that have an appeal to ordinary working people." In fact, he released the names of twenty-six people who would run on the National Front ticket along with him if he were not given a place on the ticket of the unified right. By March 1983, he added, countering allegations by the traditional right concerning the Front's lack of political clout, he would easily be able to come up with the thirteen additional names required to run a slate. Nevertheless, he said, his objective was not to run his own ticket but to join the "united opposition" and throw the left out of office. The press translated his remarks: "For M. Stirbois, the simplest solution would be a unified ticket headed by a person meeting certain requirements that he sketched in broad terms. His description readily called to mind the name of Jean Hieaux."[7]

Jean Hieaux had been first deputy mayor of Dreux under Jean Cauchon from 1965 to 1977. The owner of a local bank, which he inherited, he belonged to an upper class consisting of fewer than a dozen families, all living on two or three streets in central Dreux, all related by marriage, and, like the upper-class families of Chartres and Evreux, "more interested" (according to the demographer Michel Michel) "in office, in positions of authority and prestige, than in economic functions."[8] While still very young, Hieaux had joined the battle in Dreux against Maurice Viollette. In 1947 he became the youngest member of the city council on an RPR ticket. After 1977, however, he was not seen at any official ceremony or patriotic commemoration (including V-E Day and Armistice Day), when most of Dreux's prominent citizens gathered at the monuments honoring the city's war dead. For him, the left (which came to power in 1977) bore the mark of illegitimacy. For six years he behaved as if he were an "internal émigré," neither seeking nor receiving the endorsement of any party.

In the weeks following Stirbois's press conference, the centrist CDS, which had not participated in the RPR–National Front negotiations of 1982, made no attempt to hide their dismay. The press carried reports that the CDS was thinking of running its own slate of candidates. The rupture of the alliance between the CDS and the RPR was publicly announced at the end of November 1982. In a long article, Yves Cauchon, the son of Senator Jean Cauchon, lifted a corner of the veil drawn over discussions that had been roiling the right for the past several months: "Negotiations did take place, and it is no secret to anyone that they would have concluded satisfactorily had a problem peculiar to our city not compromised the outcome. A political force of the extreme right, pointing to results obtained in some miraculous fashion in the last cantonal election, is demanding—with the tacit support of one of the components of the opposition—to be included on the democratic slate that ought to be leading the forces for change in Dreux . . . Our city cannot become one of the places in France in which the group constituting the majority of the city council includes, under one political label, individuals honorable in themselves but willing to lend their support and backing to propositions inimical to the values that virtually all citizens of Dreux embrace." The son of the UDF[9] senator seemed to be staking out an unambiguous position: "The propositions championed by the National Front are absolutely incompatible with my own and my friends' views, and our desire for unity must not be satisfied at the price of equivocation or camouflage."[10] Was Yves Cauchon closing the door to an administrative alliance with the National Front, an alliance that might even go so far as to fuse the right and extreme-right slates before the second round of voting? In fact, he was proposing that the Front run its own slate in the first round, while in the time-honored centrist manner he awaited the outcome before committing himself to anything more.

Jean Hieaux was an outspoken proponent of a unified slate embracing all parties of the right from the UDF to the National Front. His reaction to the failure of the negotiations between the RPR and the UDF was to invite the local representatives of the RPR, the UDF, and the National Front to his home. As he later told the press, "Only M. Fontanille and M. Stirbois showed up. The bridges have been burned. I am therefore no longer a candidate, and there is no need to discuss the matter further . . . In this business two errors were made. First, the strength of my convictions and views was underestimated. The second error was made by M. Jean Cauchon, who was unwilling to listen to his former city councillors even though they had their finger on the pulse of public opinion in Dreux. The majority of voters want a fully united opposition."[11]

So it was Jean-René Fontanille who headed the combined RPR–National Front ticket, with Jean-Pierre Stirbois in the number-two spot. This slate was supported by some members of the Parti Républicain (part of the UDF alliance in the name of which Yves Cauchon had rejected a unified ticket). The UDF ran its own slate, headed by a relatively little-known physician. Cauchon ran in the number-two spot.

In addition to the slate of the incumbent left and these two right-wing slates, three other slates of candidates were placed before the voters: two from the extreme left and an "apolitical" ticket running under the banner of "Dreux–Alternative." The apoliticals included activists in various local organizations, and their sole slogan was "to deliver the city from sterile partisan debte." Although this maneuver irritated the political professionals of both right and left, it is worth noting that similar slates, based on a rejection of all traditional parties and old political rhetoric, emerged in other cities at around the same time (though unbeknownst to anyone in Dreux).

That 1983 municipal election campaign was strange indeed. Rumors flew: it was said that 800 new Turkish workers would soon arrive in the city; that the mayor was having a factory built to employ them; that the mayor had arranged for the release of the murderer of a shopping-mall security guard and had offered him a job at city hall; that the mayor would authorize the building of a mosque at Les Chamards; last but not least, that the mayor had secretly had a child by a Moroccan man and was keeping the child hidden. In addition to these wild rumors, which were not too different from those circulating at the same time in places like Roubaix, Grenoble, and Chambéry, a new form of propaganda was tried for the first time. Here is a report that appeared in *Le Nouvel Observateur* on 4 March 1983: "Over the past few days a strange group of political campaigners has descended on the Prod-'hommes section of Dreux, the poorest neighborhood in the city. These energetic spokesmen pass themselves off as salesmen and go from door to door in the projects. Their sample cases are filled with various items, all of them expensive: VCRs, hi-fi systems, jewelry. When the door opens, they greet the lady of the house: 'Good day, madam. Are you interested? No? Too bad! Your neighbor (Mohammed or Miloud or Youssef) has two of them. I'm not kidding you. Thanks to Madame Gaspard, the Arabs around here earn more than the French.' "

The Jean-Pierre Stirbois of 1983 was no longer the street fighter of 1979. The *Nouvel Observateur* article continued: "Friday, 11 February, 8:30 p.m. Big public rally on behalf of the RPR–National Front. Where are the combat fatigues, the leather jackets, the muscles, and all the paraphernalia of old? There were no more than five shaved heads in the back of the room. At the National Front convention [in 1982] Stirbois had shouted, 'Immigrants from across the Mediterranean, back to your shacks!' At this rally Stirbois, looking like a banker in polished shoes and smart trousers, expressed himself more soberly: 'The people of Dreux will defend their historical and cultural identity . . . The flow of immigration must be reversed.' "

On the left, both city officials and party activists had been oddly serene and confident until just before the launching of the official campaign. The national press praised us: Dreux was an innovative, well-run city. Yet a poll conducted in December 1982 showed that, while the citizens of Dreux were satisfied with their mayor, they were dissastisfied with the incumbent team of city officials as a whole. Immigration and crime were their paramount concerns. The extreme right had put its message across very well indeed. Forewarned by the poll results, whose implications for the left I recognized, I urged other officials to respond to the threat directly and personally. For the next three months I organized countless meetings in homes around the city. I kept a log of these visits. Number of citizens attending: more than 2,000. Issues raised spontaneously: the wretched state of stairwells, vandalism of vehicles in parking lots, animal nuisances. Not a word about immigration. No one wanted to talk about that. It was as if people had already made up their minds and were reluctant to have their convictions challenged or criticized. In order to get my audiences to discuss the problems of coexisting with foreign families, I tried to prod them: "People are saying I protect juvenile delinquents, especially if they're foreigners. Have you heard that?" My audiences were embarrassed, as if ashamed of their views but still clinging to them. On leaving I was seldom sure of having won them over.

After a tough campaign on which the views of the National Front left an indelible mark, the two extreme-left slates emerged from the first round with nearly 5 percent of the vote, the apoliticals with 5.3 percent, the unified left with a little more than 40 percent, and the UDF with 18.8 percent, far behind the RPR–National Front with nearly 31 percent.

As the first-round votes were being counted in Dreux's dance hall, news of Hubert Dubedout's defeat in Grenoble sent shock waves through the room. Left-wing groups, which had not fully mobilized against the threat, now took the measure of the danger: it was possible, it seemed, for an extreme-right-wing slate to win an election. There was an immediate surge of support for the incumbent municipal team. That support was further solidified by the announcement that the two right-wing tickets would merge: the head of the UDF ticket threw his support to the RPR–National Front ticket. The UDF fell apart over this move. Several of its candidates now joined the Fontanille slate, on which Jean-Pierre Stirbois was demoted to fifth place. Stirbois, in other words, was prepared to sacrifice himself on the altar of unity—a unity that his own shrewd tactics had helped to bring about. He won his bet: from now on he was a power to be reckoned with. The entire right accepted this. Only Yves Cauchon and a few of his allies in the CDS chose to withdraw rather than form an alliance with the extreme right. The apolitical slate, Dreux–Alternative, refused to take a position. It withdrew without advising its voters how to vote in the second round.

For a week the city had the shakes, as if it had come down with a fever. Never had an election so divided the citizens or raised passions to such a pitch. Flyers—both genuine and counterfeit—flooded the streets, which came to life at night as cars filled with poster carriers, most of whom came from other cities, wove their way among cars of officials charged with surveying their activities and journalists sent to observe the frenetic contest. The poster people fought to "hold" a water tower covered with election posters for their side or to reserve a bridge or tunnel for their use. Shots were fired.

On the night of 20 March, a crowd of 2,000 invaded the dance hall and spilled over into the adjacent square. The tension was palpable. Large numbers of immigrants and their children—the silent constituency over which the election was being fought—came down from the heights where they lived. Not daring to mix with the "native" population but avid to know who won, they stayed on the edge of the square. It took a long time to count the votes. The results hung in the balance until the last moment. In the end the left-wing slate emerged the winner—by eight votes.

"Fascism has been stopped!" On Sunday night inside the dance hall, this slogan was chanted long and loud. Outside it spurred some in the crowd to acts of vandalism: a car occupied by supporters of the Fontanille slate was damaged and windows at the local RPR headquarters were smashed during the night, as were the windows of a café whose owner was known to be an RPR activist.

On the day after the vote, the election entered its third round. A last-minute surge by the left had snatched victory from the jaws of defeat, but the margin was so narrow that the right filed a challenge before the Administrative Tribunal. It seemed likely that the election would be nullified.

At the national level, the Socialist Party seemed unsure about what attitude to adopt concerning the presence of immigrants on French soil. As I saw it at the time, this doubt seemed likely to have important implications for the future. Not only in Dreux but in many other cities, the right and extreme right had made an issue of the fact that one plank in President Mitterrand's 110-point campaign platform had been to grant the right to vote to foreign residents. In all my public appearances I supported the president's proposal. Meanwhile the government chose to remain silent on all issues related to immigration.[12]

Within the leadership of the Socialist Party, some were now proposing to take a fresh look at the whole matter of immigrants' political rights. The left was fearful. It sensed the doubts of working-class voters that I had discovered for myself in the course of my campaign. An unspoken competition was under way both in the workplace and in residential neighborhoods. Unemployment made the foreigner, especially the recently arrived foreigner, a potential rival. "Two million unemployed, two million immigrants too many." This National Front slogan, first introduced in 1982, was brought up to date (doubled) to reflect the increase in unemployment. People who felt barricaded inside their low-rent apartment buildings were more animated than ever against the North African and Turk invaders. The Socialists wished to avoid a national debate that would be uncomfortable and divisive. For a party in power, it is easier to talk about the economy than to discuss the future of society.

Given this climate, I was convinced for better or worse that I was not the best person to head the ticket in the event of a new election. In order to win, I felt, the party should choose a new local leader at once. A poll conducted a few months earlier suggested that the best choice would be a new candidate, one not involved with the previous (that is, my) administration. A local industrialist, solid, reassuring, and warm-hearted, agreed to step in. So I announced that I was no longer a candidate for mayor and nominated Marcel Piquet to succeed me. On 20 March 1983 the party agreed to accept the new candidate.

On 2 June a hearing officer at the Administrative Tribunal of Orléans announced that the judges had found a discrepancy of seven between the number of voters checked off on registration lists and the number of votes counted. In a long series of precedents, the courts had ruled that votes not checked off on the lists should be subtracted from the winner's total. "If precedent were to be overturned, the present occasion would be ideal, because the seven individuals in question did in fact vote, but such a ruling would threaten the foundations on which electoral legitimacy rests."[13] Even deducting those seven votes, the left-wing ticket still would have won by a single vote—had not one absentee ballot been voided by the court. The outcome was a tie. The hearing officer recommended that the election be nullified, and the judges so ruled.

The new mayor, Marcel Piquet, did not appeal this judgment to the higher Council of State. His view, which I shared, was that to do so would prolong an ugly situation for no purpose. It seemed unlikely that the council would go against the weight of so many legal precedents, and Dreux would probably find itself in the same mess some months later. New elections were therefore scheduled for September.

A Fifth Political Force

Since March the "Dreux affair" was an embarrassment for the right, especially the RPR, at the national level. Jacques Chirac, the party's leader and mayor of Paris, was questioned several times by journalists about the alliance his party had forged with the National Front in the small Eure-et-Loir city. On Radio Europe 1's *Press Club* of 30 January 1983, Chirac was categorical: "I, for one, have no relation of any kind with a movement based on principles that I am fighting against." On the eve of the first round, Chirac appeared on Radio-Communauté, a station affiliated with the Jewish community of Paris. When questioned again about the situation in Dreux, he replied with some annoyance: "I have personally requested that this slate not be granted the official approval of the RPR. I repeat, I personally have made this demand. In my eyes those people have a congenital defect: they are racists." But Chirac's remarks did not stop Jean-René Fontanille from claiming the backing of the RPR, and when he was asked about his relations with national party headquarters, he responded: "Look, before taking a decision like this, we obviously got a green light from the national leadership."[14]

The nullification of the March election left the situation as it was before. The RPR asked its local forces to refrain from entering into an alliance with Jean-Pierre Stirbois. Undeterred, Stirbois put up his own slate for the race, certain he would have to be reckoned with in the second round. He said he hoped to obtain at least 15 percent of the vote—a figure that made people smile.

Exit Jean-René Fontanille, the all-too-visible embodiment of the "March mistake" of collaborating with the National Front and breaking the alliance with the CDS. Jean Hieaux, who a few months earlier had agreed to participate in the election only if the right allied itself with the extreme right, now changed his mind and agreed to head a joint RPR–UDF ticket from which the National Front was excluded. This time there would be only three slates of candidates in the first round of the elections: a left-wing slate headed by Marcel Piquet, a right-wing slate headed by Jean Hieaux, and a National Front slate headed by Jean-Pierre Stirbois.

Because the new campaign was shorter and took place during the summer vacation months, it was less vitriolic than the earlier go-round. On 4 September the results came in: Hieaux, 42.7 percent; Piquet, 40.6 percent; Stirbois, 16.7 percent. Depending on which side you were on, the figures were reason for appalled consternation or triumphant joy. Shouts of "Fascism shall not pass!" vied with cries of "Stirbois to city hall!" There was fighting in the streets. On the right the concern was less with street brawls than with how to prepare for the second round of voting.

The left had nowhere to turn for votes other than from those who had abstained in the first round. In March the right and extreme-right slates had together won 49 percent of the first-round vote; this time they took 60 percent. To be sure, voter participation was down 4 percent from the first round in March and 9 percent down from the second round. But the left had no one to negotiate with, and a ten-point deficit is impossible to overcome in a week.

In March the RPR–National Front alliance in Dreux attracted little attention among journalists preoccupied with municipal elections across France. On 4 September, however, the Dreux by-election was the political event of the season. For days Dreux was flooded with reporters. The National Front's total of nearly 17 percent in the first round—a level never before achieved by any extreme-right-wing party in France—was front-page news across the country. When it was announced the same day that the RPR–UDF ticket would ally with the National Front ticket in the second round, national leaders were taken by surprise. That night, when Simone Veil appeared on the television program *Moment of Truth,* she was quickly asked how she would vote on Sunday if she were a resident of Dreux. After a moment's hesitation she answered, "I would abstain." Over the next week, the right could reach no agreement on how to respond. Some leaders, such as Jacques Chaban-Delmas and Olivier Stirn, rejected any form of compromise with the extreme right. Stirn actually abandoned the right over this issue, and three years later he joined the Socialist Party. But others, including Jean Lecanuet, Bernard Pons, François Léotard, Dominique Baudis, Alain Carrignon, and Jean-Pierre Soisson, signed an appeal to vote for the unified Hieaux ticket, an appeal that was published in full-page ads in regional newspapers.

On the left some militants, particularly the younger ones, were determined to fight. They were also determined to reveal to the nation as a whole the nature of a disease that, having attacked

Dreux, could soon spread elsewhere. They hoped to arouse wide-spread indignation by denouncing the alliance just forged on the right, for they were convinced that the danger was by no means confined to Dreux and that the incorporation of the extreme right into the political process was a matter of major significance. On the Monday morning after the election, Simone Signoret called a number of her friends and formed a committee. Her husband Yves Montand refused to join, however, owing to the presence of Communists on Marcel Piquet's slate, and his refusal attracted considerable publicity. But such prominent personalities as Simone de Beauvoir, Jean Cassou, Claude Mauriac, Eugène Descamp, Alexandre Minkowski, and Bernard Kouchner announced their support for the left-wing ticket. A demonstration was planned for the eve of the voting in Dreux. More than 2,000 people were invited, including a number of government ministers, national officials of antiracist organizations, writers, and artists. In the heart of Dreux, Daniel Gélin was to read an appeal from Claude Mauriac.

On 11 September, in a very tense climate, the unified ticket of right and extreme right won with 55.3 percent of the vote. National television broadcast live pictures of riot police charging into a crowd of people hurling rocks and shouting "Fascism shall not pass!" But it had passed. Jean-Pierre Stirbois became deputy mayor of Dreux. Of the eleven other members of his first-round ticket who had been included in the unified ticket on the second round, three, himself included, became deputy mayors. It was the first time that the National Front, operating in the open, had won an election.

The Dreux Vote Is Confirmed

In Dreux the upcoming June 1984 elections to the European parliament aroused little excitement. The only locals to take to the streets were those employed by the various parties to hang election posters. Political rallies at the subprefecture were sparsely attended. Yet when the National Front announced that it would hold a rally in Dreux, leftist groups quickly issued a flurry of press releases announcing demonstrations. Things heated up quickly. Although

Jean-Pierre Stirbois had been seen in Dreux infrequently since his election, the policies of the municipal government bore all the earmarks of extremist influence: leftists were eliminated from government posts; the local library canceled its subscription to the satirical weekly *Le Canard enchaîné* and the magazine *Europe;* certain exhibitions were canceled on grounds of left-wing bias. The municipal theater staged a play by Henry de Montherlant, to which the deputy mayor for cultural affairs, a National Front militant, invited his political allies on city-hall stationery; the play failed anyway, despite the attempt to fill the theater with a rightist claque. The Dreux School of Music, which as it happens was headed by a left-wing militant, became the target of attacks on waste. Finally, housing allowances were suspended for schoolteachers found cohabiting with partners to whom they were not married; the investigations were conducted at dawn by sheriff's deputies dispatched to the scene of the crime.

The National Front rally in Dreux led to further violence. One local journalist was severely beaten by National Front bodyguards. The city police were accused of failing to come to the aid of people in danger. The extreme right denied all responsibility. Local people blamed extremists on both sides, left and right. The problem, they said, was not rightist troublemakers but politics in general. Meanwhile Stirbois remained above suspicion as an honorable deputy mayor.

The European elections of 1984 revealed that the National Front had risen to unprecedented heights nationwide with 11 percent of the total vote, a share as large as that of the Communist Party. In Dreux Le Pen's slate received 21.8 percent of the vote, or 4 percent more than in September 1983.

The National Front Moves On

It was once again time for cantonal elections. In Dreux only one seat was up for reelection: the one representing the canton that included the town of Vernouillet, whose incumbent was the Socialist Maurice Legendre (last reelected in 1982). In this election

Legendre was forced into second-round balloting for the first time in his political career. The National Front received 17.5 percent of the first-round vote (and as much as 18 percent in some districts of Dreux).

By 1986 the political climate had changed dramatically since the days of the *chambre rose*, when the socialists enjoyed an absolute majority in the National Assembly. Economic austerity had borne bitter fruit. Left-wing voters were gloomy, and the right was up in arms. Proportional representation had been introduced by a desperate left-wing majority. Because of this, the National Front could not expect to win a seat in the Eure-et-Loir despite its significant vote in the département. So Jean-Pierre Stirbois temporarily focused his efforts elsewhere, heading his party's slate in the Hauts-de-Seine, where he was soon elected deputy. He entrusted his wife with the job of heading the ticket in the Eure-et-Loir. (She also headed a slate of candidates in the regional elections, which were held the same day.) The Front failed to elect a deputy from the Eure-et-Loir. In Dreux it received 16.1 percent of the vote, or less than Le Pen had obtained in the 1984 European elections. The campaign was relatively subdued. Marie-France Stirbois presented herself as a dynamic businesswoman and mother. Always smiling, the candidate made frequent appearances at markets, where she handed out flyers.

The local press did not focus its scrutiny on the National Front during the campaign. People had become used to the Lepenist presence on the political scene: it was just another political party, like all the rest. By contrast, the split within the RPR was page-one news in the region for several weeks. To everyone's surprise, the national leadership of the party did not tap Martial Taugourdeau, the former deputy who had been elected president of the Conseil Général in 1985, to head its ticket, thus ending nearly a century of Radical domination of politics in the département. Instead the RPR leadership, responding to a national agreement with the CNIP, sought to force the local RPR to accept Michel Junot, the secretary-general of the CNIP, as its top candidate.

A few months earlier, the RPR had moved to replace its former local leader, Jean-René Fontanille, who had tired of politics, with a young man well known to students of the French extreme right: Alain Robert. Robert was the founder of three extremist groups: the Occident movement, the GUD, and Ordre Nouveau. He had been a member of the National Front's leadership committee in 1972. He was also a founder of the Parti des Forces Nouvelles, a former secretary of the CNIP, and had run, with RPR support, as the CNIP candidate in the March 1985 cantonal elections in Seine-Saint-Denis. This same Robert, who had just joined Jacques Chirac's RPR, was described in a 1968 police report as "looking more like the idol of a gang of juvenile delinquents than a political leader."[15] Besides having been associated with a number of extreme-right-wing movements, he was an old acquaintance of Jean-Pierre Stirbois's. Both joined the National Front in 1972, but Robert, deemed a loose cannon by the party's leader, was expelled in 1973 despite his being a founding member.

Had RPR party leaders decided, from their Paris headquarters, to go after the National Front vote in Eure-et-Loir by dispatching Alain Robert to recruit candidates likely to appeal to voters drawn to the extreme right? Had they come to the conclusion that Taugourdeau (who had backed Michel Debré in the 1981 presidential election) was not the best man to recover the lost sheep that had strayed from the flock in response to Le Pen's populist rhetoric? In any case Michel Junot, who in 1984 stated that the CNIP "has no doctrinal enemies on the right" and that he could "not understand why certain other party leaders want to exclude a movement like the National Front," was now assigned the task of poaching on one of the favorite hunting grounds of the very same National Front.

The RPR was trying out a new strategy. But it underestimated the reaction of various leaders of the local right, who disliked any interference from Paris. The local UDF and RPR formed a common front against the intruder. Taugourdeau, hurt by his party's rejection and convinced that it was a political blunder, joined forces with the UDF. His judgment proved correct. Across the département the Junot slate captured only 8.3 percent of the vote. The UDF slate, led by Maurice Dousset with Taugourdeau in the number-two spot, finished second, with 27 percent, enough to elect two of its candidates under the rules of proportional representation. The split on the right allowed the Socialist Party to capture the other two seats.

Realignments and Ruptures

On 14 May 1988, after reelection to the presidency, Mitterrand dissolved the National Assembly that had been elected in March 1986. In the interim, Jacques Chirac as prime minister had eliminated proportional representation in favor of election of deputies by district in the wake of a redistricting carried out by interior minister Charles Pasqua (also a member of Chirac's RPR) in November 1986. The Eure-et-Loir département now comprised four electoral districts.

In 1981 the Socialists had tried "parachuting" an outsider into the Eure-et-Loir's second district.[16] In 1988 there were no parachutists in sight; the skies remained desperately empty. Socialist leaders at the national level, hard pressed to find safe districts, analyzed the results district by district. The remapped Dreux district did not look good. Mitterrand had won 52 percent of the vote on 8 May, but the combined parties of the left had scored only 39 percent in 1986. And if there is anything a parachutist does not want, it is to land in an unsafe district.

As the twice-elected incumbent deputy, it fell to me to represent the Socialist Party. At the local convention that met to choose a candidate, I was the only contender for the nomination.

In 1986 the right was divided. Now it was the left's turn to parade its disarray before the voters. In their long-standing battle for influence, the Socialists had gradually supplanted the Radicals. In politics the closer competitors are, the more competitive they become—they must compete for the same voters. In 1986, however, old quarrels seemed to have been laid to rest: in that year the

Socialists and the Left Radicals of the MRG ran a common slate, and two MRG candidates were elected to the Regional Council. Unfortunately, one of the successful candidates believed that the third legislative district of Eure-et-Loir, comprising the city of Nogent-le-Rotrou, was to be reserved for him.

For obscure reasons, the MRG's claims on this seat found support within the Eure-et-Loir Socialist Federation. When the pro-MRG faction failed to have its way, its disappointed members sowed discord by urging the national party to parachute outsiders into the district to eliminate the candidate nominated by the local party organization. These attempts failed, however, and the local Socialist candidate was the only one authorized to represent the presidential majority. The matter was not laid to rest, however: the Radical whose hopes had been disappointed chose to run for the seat in Nogent-le-Rotrou anyway, and he received behind-the-scenes support from certain leading Socialists. In two of the département's three other districts, including the Dreux district, other Radicals did the same.

During the campaign, some Socialists (including the wife of the mayor of Chartres, a man who had served as a government minister under Socialist prime ministers Pierre Mauroy and Laurent Fabius) urged voters to vote for the Radical candidate in the third district. Despite this support, the Socialist candidate was elected deputy on 21 June. In the Dreux district, the MRG candidate obtained only 3 percent of the vote. But the dissension had opened a wound in the Socialist Party, part of which actively supported the Radical candidate.

In the first round, the Socialist candidate received 38 percent of the vote in the city of Dreux, compared with 4.4 percent for the MRG candidate. For the first time the Communists were also divided: a reform candidate supported by various leftist groups received 2.3 percent of the vote, which reduced the total of the official Communist Party candidate to below the 5 percent cutoff. Martial Taugourdeau obtained 32.7 percent, Marie-France Stirbois 17.7 percent. The candidate of the extreme right was thereby eliminated from the second round.

Taugourdeau was then elected deputy with 55.8 percent of the vote. In Dreux the left fell just 111 votes short of a majority. Charles Pasqua's redistricting had accomplished its purpose. The dissension within the Socialist Party had done the rest.

Traditionally, voter turnout is lower in cantonal elections than in national or municipal elections. But the unprecedented lack of voter interest throughout France in the September 1988 cantonal elections was said to be a result of the unusual number of elections held in 1988. In Dreux, where two seats held by the RPR since 1982 were up for reelection, two-thirds of the voters stayed home. The National Front ran a deputy mayor of Dreux for one seat and a young campaign staffer for the other. The two candidates received, respectively, 18.4 and 11.8 percent of the votes cast. In the second round, Socialist Maurice Ravanne beat the right-wing candidate to take the seat for West Dreux.

On 9 November Jean-Pierre Stirbois attended a rally in Dreux calling for a "no" vote on the referendum concerning the status of New Caledonia. Driving alone back home to Neuilly at two in the morning, he was killed in a car crash.

The Matignon Experiment

New municipal elections were scheduled for March 1989. Five slates were in contention in the first round. The incumbent mayor, Jean Hieaux, headed the RPR–UDF ticket. Marie-France Stirbois, sensing that her party was gathering momentum and determined to demonstrate its strength, headed the National Front ticket. Once again the *gauchistes* (extreme-left splinter groups) were intent on making themselves heard. The new ingredient in the mix was the division of the Socialists, who appeared on two slates. Along with the official Socialist-Communist slate headed by new *conseiller général* Maurice Ravanne, there was also a slate that called itself Autrement (literally, Otherwise), a successor to the apolitical slate that had run in the March 1983 municipal election.

137

This ticket was headed by a Socialist dissident who had failed to win the nomination of his party section. The final position on the Autrement ticket was filled by Marcel Piquet, the losing Socialist candidate in September 1983. The rest of the ticket included roughly a dozen Socialists, mostly supporters of Prime Minister Rocard, some CDS dissidents, a number of social-service professionals, including a former RPR candidate, a few Radicals, and even a man who had run on the National Front slate in 1983. The new ticket's slogan was "No to the parties." Owing to the diverse background of the candidates, who had forged an alliance for electoral purposes only, it was impossible for the Autrement slate to claim the backing of the presidential majority. That fact did not stop them from claiming on the stump that they were following in *my* footsteps. Privately, moreover, they put out the word that they enjoyed the support of people in high places. Matignon—the palace where the prime minister has his offices—was said to be keeping a close eye on this race.

The division among the Socialists attracted more attention than the candidacy of Marie-France Stirbois, who was now a familiar fixture of the local political scene. The left was in disarray. Campaign workers were frantic. Voters were not sure whether to be perplexed, discouraged, or disgusted. Many threatened to stay home or even to send the left a warning by voting for the National Front.

On 10 March 1989 Jean Hieaux received 34 percent of the votes cast. Maurice Ravanne's Communist-Socialist slate finished second with 22.7 percent, just nosing out the Stirbois slate, which had 22.2 percent. Autrement came in fourth with 19.1 percent, and the *gauchistes* had 2 percent.

The question that arose prior to the second round of voting was whether the Ravanne and Autrement slates would merge. Together they had received 41.8 percent of the vote, and they might win in a three-way contest (left versus right versus extreme right). In contrast to 1983, the mayor of Dreux this time made no attempt to conclude a pact with the National Front. Instead he wagered that the three other slates would all stand pat. His equanimity suggests that he had allies inside Autrement who he knew would hold out to the end against any attempt to merge the tickets. It was a risk, but a calculated one, and in the end the dissident Socialists ran true to form. The Socialist federation in Dreux, having vainly called for negotiations, asked me to approach the staff of Prime Minister Rocard. My calls were not returned. Journalists who questioned members of Rocard's staff about the situation in Dreux have told me that one official close to the prime minister said, "We are conducting an experiment in Dreux." If so, it was a strange experiment, and a strange place to choose for it.

Only the *gauchistes* were eliminated by the results of the first round. Hence in the second round four slates were still in the running—an unprecedented situation. In the meantime Autrement slate had picked up the support of the Socialist deputy who was also the mayor of Chartres (this time he chose not to rely on his wife to make his sentiments known), the mayor of Vernouillet, the former Socialist deputy Maurice Legendre, and the CDS senator Jean Cauchon. These and other prominent local leaders published a glossy brochure calling on Dreux voters to reject "any compromise with the political parties." It was a depressing concession to the ideology of the moment on the part of men who owed their careers to political parties. The muddle was complete. Still the support of prominent Socialists for the dissident ticket changed nothing; the final order of finish was the same as in the first round.

Although the incumbent mayor received only 37.5 percent of the vote, his ticket won an absolute majority of the seats on the city council, thus assuring him of remaining in power until 1995. Marie-France Stirbois failed in both rounds to obtain as many votes as Le Pen had received in the 1988 presidential elections. In percentage terms, however, she scored the best results that the National Front had ever achieved in Dreux.

The Matignon experiment was conclusive in at least one respect: an attempt to reach out to right-wing voters can easily lead to confusion that benefits the right and fosters the growth of the extreme right, to say nothing of causing voters to shun the polls in droves.

A Third Force in the City

When Le Pen offered Marie-France Stirbois a low-ranking place on the National Front's slate of candidates for the European parliament, one that offered her little hope of being elected, she declined to run. In Dreux the campaign unfolded without incident. There was no need for the ritual protest that the left, the extreme left, and various human-rights groups organized whenever Le Pen came to town: he stayed away.

The voter turnout was low: 42.3 percent. In Dreux the ticket led by former president Valéry Giscard d'Estaing received 27 percent of the vote. The Socialist ticket led by former prime minister Laurent Fabius (22 percent) outpolled the Le Pen ticket by only seventy-five votes. The slate headed by former health minister Simone Veil received just 8 percent. With 21.6 percent of the vote, the National Front had become the third-ranking political force in the city.

Martial Taugourdeau, deputy for Eure-et-Loir's second legislative district, was elected to the Senate in September 1989, necessitating yet another election to choose his replacement as deputy. Michel Lethuiller, who was serving as *conseiller général* for one of Dreux's cantons, was the RPR candidate. As we saw earlier, in 1982 Lethuiller was among those responsible for negotiating with Jean-Pierre Stirbois between rounds of the cantonal elections. As mayor of a town near Dreux, he also offered municipal facilities to the National Front and its friends so that they could celebrate their entry into Dreux's city government, on 11 September, 1983.

I was not a candidate in the race for deputy. Several months earlier, Dreux's Socialist Party section had alerted national headquarters to the likelihood that there would be a legislative by-election in the second district. Section leaders wanted to know what the leadership's position was and whether or not there were plans to parachute an outside candidate into the race. But no response was forthcoming—national headquarters did not issue a single directive. When local party activists gathered to choose a candidate, they were not unmindful of the devastating effects of internal dissension and therefore chose to mollify the dissidents. As their nominee they chose my former adjunct, Claude Nespoulous, a Socialist who had been a supporter of Pierre Mendès France and who was acceptable to all factions of the party. As candidate for the position of adjunct deputy, they chose a doctor who happened to be the son-in-law of the Socialist mayor of Vernouillet, one of the prominent party officials who had shown sympathy for the dissident ticket in the municipal elections.

The Communist Party's traditional candidate was also on the hustings, along with a dissident Gaullist and a Green environmentalist. To complicate matters still further, an MRG militant joined the race at the last moment, although the Socialists had hoped that their candidate would enjoy the united support of the non-Communist left. The MRG candidate, who had run in March on the Autrement ticket, was none other than the son of the mayor of Vernouillet. Things were in such a muddle that a mother cat would have lost her kittens.

The candidacy of Marie-France Stirbois was not unexpected. The campaign proceeded without open provocations or violence. The National Front candidate cultivated a proper manner both in her own appearance and in her campaign literature. Her statements, while resolutely right-wing, carefully avoided inflammatory language.

Voters nevertheless received, from anonymous sources, some rather strange items in the mail. One was a copy of a letter sloppily typed, liked the notorious Mustapha letter, on a poor typewriter. It began: "We, Algerians and Arabs, inform the Judeo-French population: more than anything else we hate France and its people, jewified to the very marrow." And it ended: "France is already ours: we have occupied it since our victory in 1962, as is only natural. Didn't the Germans occupy France in 1940 after their

victory? The difference is that we Muslim Arabs are going to occupy it PERMANENTLY thanks to the children our women are pro-
ducing here in large numbers, while you pay for them . . . Chirac
said, 'France is a Muslim power.' We will bugger that pig Le Pen
in Paris' Notre Dame cathedral, which soon will number among
our 779 mosques from Perpignan to Dunkirk." The letter was of
course unsigned, and no one knew where it had originated. Then
two high-school students were questioned for distributing a flyer
outside their school. The text, signed by the "Groupe Action
Nationaliste Français," concluded: "Jews, bolsheviks, Muslims—
rotten filth. A disgusted France vomits you up." The case was
closed without further action.

Another flyer, this one elegantly printed and bearing the imprint
of the "Association Nationale pour l'Intégration des Immigrés du
Tiers Monde, Secteur Seine-Saint-Denis, 75585 Paris CEDEX 12,"
was also widely distributed in the district. It called upon residents
to report vacant housing in their neighborhood in order to permit
the relocation of immigrant families with large numbers of children presently housed in poor conditions. These families were to
be moved to Dreux and Vernouillet. The document went on to
explain that immigrant access to housing would be facilitated
thanks to the "bill filed by the Honorable Michel Hannoun, deputy (RPR)," indicating further that this bill had been "approved by
a majority of the Assembly (Communists, Socialists, RPR, and UDF)
and would be enforced despite the Le Pen group's reactionary and
racist opposition." Investigation revealed that no such association
existed, but voters who received the flyer didn't know that.

This time around, the regional press was preoccupied with dissension on the right. If the Socialist left in the département had
been in crisis since the 1988 legislative elections, the right was in
no better shape. It too was deeply divided. The senatorial elections
of September 1989 had provoked an internal struggle in the ranks
of the local UDF, with the RPR acting as arbiter. Although the UDF
did not run a candidate in the legislative by-election, it declined to
offer its support to the RPR candidate. Maurice Dousset, the local

UDF leader, chose to remain silent and refused to attend the RPR's election-eve rally. So there were divisions and scores to be settled on the right as well as the left. Voters found these intrigues difficult to comprehend.

Marie-France Stirbois, whose very active campaign was closely followed by the press, could therefore be certain that one of her party's central issues would strike a resonant chord: the "Gang of Four" (as the National Front referred to the four leading parties: Communists, Socialists, RPR, UDF) was so taken up with political bickering, according to Le Pen, that it had lost contact with the concerns of ordinary French men and women. But the one question that seemed to interest the media most was whether Stirbois would win the votes of more than 12.5 percent of those registered to vote in the district (as required in order to go on to the second round). If so, would she remain in the race even if that meant facilitating a Socialist victory? Not for a moment did anyone imagine that the RPR or Socialist candidates might not make it to the second round.

On 26 November, to everyone's astonishment, Marie-France Stirbois was the only candidate to win the votes of more than 12.5 percent of those registered. Fewer than one of every two registered voters had gone to the polls. The National Front candidate finished far out in front of her opponents with 42.5 percent of the vote. The RPR candidate, who received 24.6 percent, had mobilized only one out of ten registered voters. The Socialist candidate, with 18.1 percent, represented only 7.8 percent of the electorate. The previously unknown Green candidate finished with 4.9 percent of the vote, ahead of the MRG with 4.2 percent and the Communist, who dropped below 4 percent. The dissident Gaullist claimed only 2 percent.

Under the law, a run-off election was required, since only one candidate had qualified for the second round. In run-off elections in Dreux it was traditionally the Socialist who came out ahead, but this time Stirbois took 49 percent of the vote (within the city) and the Socialist came in third with only 15.3 percent, trailing both the

National Front and the RPR. Accordingly, the Socialist candidate was eliminated (as was the Socialist candidate in Marseilles, which was also holding a legislative by-election). The RPR candidate qualified for the second round because the law required at least two candidates.

On 3 December Marie-France Stirbois was elected deputy with 61.3 percent of the vote districtwide. In Dreux, more than four out of ten voters stayed home, nearly one in ten cast a blank or void ballot, and three in ten voted for the National Front.

An Extremist City?

Six years earlier, on the day after the first round of voting in 1983, many people had gone to Dreux's marketplace to express their shock and ask one another how it could have happened. Which of the customers in the market could have voted for the fascists? It was not easy to pick out the one voter in ten capable of such an act. Everyone had ideas and suspicions, but who could know for sure? Few of the National Front's supporters boasted of their vote publicly for fear of incurring the disapproval of their neighbors.

By December 1989, however, those who voted for Marie-France Stirbois were no longer afraid to show themselves. When your candidate takes 60 percent of the vote, you are proud to be on the winning side. National Front activists now felt at ease in public. Those who voted for the extreme right no longer concealed their identity.

Who does vote for the National Front in Dreux?[17] It may seem foolish even to ask the question given the results of the 1989 election. When a party receives 60 percent of the vote, it has to be drawing voters from all segments of the population. This means that when you walk down the street, shop in a store, or go to a dinner party, you are inevitably meeting people who voted for Marie-France Stirbois. One in three registered voters is a lot of people. The idea that such a vote could have been an accident or a momentary enthusiasm cannot withstand scrutiny. A party that only a few years earlier had been so insignificant as to pass almost unseen came close to obtaining a majority in the first round of an election in a French city of some 30,000 people. A party whose ideas placed it outside the bounds of ordinary politics had outpolled all the others, and this despite its leader's penchant for provocative verbal excess: Jean-Marie Le Pen had referred to the Holocaust as a mere "detail" and made an obnoxious pun on the last name of Socialist minister Michel Durafour (referring to him as "Durafour crématoire," alluding once again to the Holocaust and its crematory ovens, or *fours crématoires*).

Until the National Front entered the political scene in the late 1970s, Dreux's political geography was simple and without surprises: the center of town voted for the right, the heights for the left. An analysis of the vote in three key precincts can help us to understand the evolution of voter behavior.

Dreux's fourth precinct is located in the center of the city. Voter turnout there was traditionally high, and the left generally fared rather poorly. It was here that Dreux's old families voted, its leading merchants and industrial executives. In 1977 I remember watching as the votes were counted in this precinct. We calculated that if the left-wing slate that I headed did better than 34 percent here, it would win a majority citywide. As it happened, we got 37 percent of the vote in the fourth precinct, an indication that we would win by a landslide, and that is how things turned out: we captured 54.8 percent of the vote overall.

The tenth precinct did not exist prior to 1973. This is the polling place for the blue- and white-collar workers who live in the high-rises at Les Chamards and the projects at La Croix Tiennac. The left counts this as a safe precinct, particularly since many of its organizers, union activists, and other sympathizers live in the area. In 1973 the Socialist candidate took 63 percent of the vote in the legislative election.

The fifteenth precinct serves the residents of the Prod'homme project. This was long the bastion of the Communist Party. In the 1967 legislative election it was the "reddest" precinct in the city, with the Communists' 36 percent putting them 12 points ahead of the SFIO (the predecessor to the Socialist Party). In the 1973 legislative election this was still the precinct in which the Communists did best (29 percent), but the vote had begun to shift toward the Socialists, who now finished only one point behind. In the second round the left scored a clear majority: 66 percent of the vote.

In 1979, when the National Front burst onto the local scene as its candidate captured 9 percent of the vote, the extreme right was still embarked on a trek through the desert as far as national political influence was concerned. In 1982, with offices up for reelection in 1,945 cantons throughout France, the extreme right managed to field only 65 candidates. In Dreux's two cantons, however, its performance was such that the 1979 results could no longer be considered an accident.[18]

The National Front received 10 percent of the vote in the fourth precinct, 13.5 percent in the tenth precinct, and 19.5 percent in the fifteenth precinct. A hasty interpretation of these results might lead to the conclusion that the extremist vote came mainly from the working class and that there had been an important shift of support from the Communist Party to the National Front. The CP was indeed in decline. Compared with the previous cantonal elections it had lost 5 points in the fourth, 6 points in the tenth, and nearly 17 points in the fifteenth precinct. But the decline of the Communists began before the emergence of the National Front. As early as the June 1981 legislative election, during which Jean-Pierre Stirbois made a miserable showing in Dreux, the Communist vote had already collapsed. The theory that working-class votes shifted from one extreme of the political spectrum to the other is not enough to account for the rise of the extreme right. Between 1981 and 1982 the left as a whole lost 8 percent in the fourth, nearly 9 percent in the tenth, and 10 percent in the fifteenth precinct, and these losses were incurred mainly by the Socialists. Having enticed a significant share of the vote away from the Communist Party between 1973 and 1981, the Socialist Party proved unable to hold on to its new electorate. In fact, a series of major voting shifts seems to have occurred in the late 1970s and early 1980s.

For a long time the differences in voting patterns between the precincts on the heights and those of central Dreux appeared to reflect the differences between two distinct subsocieties. The emergence and growing strength of the National Front changed the relation between sociology and politics. In December 1989 the old left-right geographical distinctions remained, but the gap between center and heights had narrowed. In addition, Stirbois voters were more evenly distributed across the city. For every 100 registered voters, 30 went to the polls to vote for the National Front in the fourth precinct, 25 in the tenth, and 32 in the fifteenth. The old differences had all but vanished. The mobilization of the extremist vote was virtually identical in working-class and well-to-do precincts; indeed, it was higher in the city's most "bourgeois" precinct than in its most "immigrant" one.

In 1989 central Dreux was still a bourgeois neighborhood. Among its taciturn community leaders were some who had never concealed their admiration for Marshal Pétain. The conservatism of some long-time residents was in fact heightened by a sense of being surrounded by newcomers. Then there were the young executives who had paid good money for a fancy apartment and wondered if property values would hold up. In Prod'homme, the old school principal, once an active Communist, had long since retired to the south of France. The Socialist Party, which during its years in opposition had picked up many former Communist voters, did not turn those voters into party activists. The last native French family—which also happened to represent the last active socialist presence—was gone from Les Chamards. And the Communist Party had long since ceased to be an integrating force. Dreux's working-class neighborhoods now resembled the neighborhoods of north Marseilles described by Anne Tristan, in which the National Front supplanted the Communists by providing not a new organizational framework but a common rhetoric, the rhetoric of protest, or simply a cry for help.[19]

But where were the militants of the National Front? Tristan came to know some of them in Marseilles. She discovered how they had been able to restore neighborhood meeting places and a spirit of conviviality, even if the subject of conversation at their banquets and parties was exclusion. In Dreux the National Front was like a phantom. Few party activists had been identified. Yet the party had managed to carve out a voting bloc for itself, and it could no longer be said that its vote was volatile. Its rise did not take place overnight. Over a period of twelve years, the National Front ran candidates in each of fourteen elections. Nearly every time it obtained more votes than before. In eleven years and nine months, its share of the vote rose from 2 to 61 percent, from 307 to 4,716 votes.

Its rise was irresistible—and exemplary.

Rediscovering the Citizen

The preceding pages retrace the singular history that arises from the interaction—by its very essence unique—between a place and its inhabitants. Beyond what is unique to Dreux, however, we begin to perceive the outlines of issues that all of France must face as the twentieth century draws to a close. They are the problems of a society that is sick in the same way that a living organism can be sick: society too has its symptoms and sudden fevers and requires treatment tailored to the disease.

A City Like Many Others

The growth of Dreux's population between 1954 and 1974 precipitated a crisis in the city. It was happening all across France: population growth coupled with rapid urbanization. According to Guy Burgel, "the simultaneous increase in both the population growth rate and the rate of urbanization resulted in a sharp increase in the urban population. In the two decades from 1954 to 1975 cities with populations above 5,000 gained in population by 13 million, compared with just 6 million in the period 1911–1954."[1] The list of towns whose character changed dramatically includes Vitrolles and Bois-d'Arcy, Istres and Trappes, Martigues and Creil, to name only a few. Some medium-sized cities grew less abruptly, but many towns became cities and many small cities grew into moderately large ones, with growth rates over three or four decades even more spectacular than Dreux's: Clichy-sous-Bois, whose population was 4,500 in 1965, is today a city of 28,000. Like Dreux, other communities suffered during these years from a rapid turnover in population: "A city like Evreux in Normandy," Burgel remarks, "typifies the turbulence of urban growth, a turbulence due both to the failure to retain its population and to the intensity of demographic renewal. A third of the people who lived in Evreux in 1968 were no longer there in 1975, at which time half of the population consisted of new immigrants."[2]

Meanwhile, for the past fifteen years, the dilapidated housing projects on the heights of Dreux have been the theater of clashes between sharply contrasting life styles, dietary habits, and religious practices. Discouraged adults have had to contend with unemployed youths brimming over with vitality and nowhere to go. In this respect Dreux is no different from many other places. In late 1989 the government estimated that some 400 urban neighborhoods throughout France were in need of urgent attention. These places have similar names, evocative of the fields, meadows, and woods so recently swallowed up by urban development: Les Bosquets (The Copse) in Montfermeil, Les Pâquerettes (The Daisies) in Nanterre, Le Clos des Roses (The Rose Garden) in Compiègne. In prettily named Chanteloup-les-Vignes, juvenile gangs do battle with gangs from nearby Achères in the fields and vacant lots that separate the two towns. Suddenly and without warning, a riot erupted in the Val-du-Taureau section of Vaulx-en-Velin in October 1990. As the very names suggest, new towns went up in what had been woods and farmland. Overnight, cow pastures filled with high-rises, block housing, and even a few buildings of bold design, such as the architect's dream conceived by Emile Aillaud in Grigny. The devastated remains of the once-new housing projects that ring so many of France's cities are a frightening spectacle, a nightmare to the people who live in them as well as to their elected representatives. More than one outraged visitor has been heard to exclaim that "to build a place like that was a crime."

No one has yet been held accountable for the consequences of such lethal city planning. Many of those responsible continue to pursue careers in government. As far as centralized planning is concerned, there has been surprising continuity in France from one regime to another. It was the government of Vichy that decided in 1943 to "nationalize" city planning by setting up an office responsible for rethinking the problems of urban design and overseeing urban development. From then on, even the most insignificant local renovation plan had to be submitted to the national government for approval. After the Liberation this system remained in place. Indeed, postwar reconstruction, followed by a severe housing shortage and the discovery of scandalous conditions in conglomerates of makeshift shacks *(bidonvilles)*, made people believe that comprehensive urban planning was an absolute necessity. Plan succeeded plan, as housing projects and new cities of various descriptions went up at the government's behest. Since the government held the purse strings, moreover, it established the rules governing construction methods, permissible density, and building characteristics. Although the goals of government planning were certainly generous, the appropriated financing was inadequate to realize them. The state's modernizing ambitions actually ran afoul of the laws of the marketplace. In the late 1960s, when Gaston Defferre, the mayor of Marseilles, called for the city to assume ownership of all land within its borders in order to combat "spatial segregation," some branded him a dangerous revolutionary while others dismissed him as a harmless dreamer. When the left came to power in 1981, it was careful to disassociate itself from any such revolutionary goal. Successive governments embodied their respective visions of the city in new zoning codes and redevelopment programs. Market forces did the rest: buildings went up where land was cheap, far from existing urban centers. The least wealthy and least fortunate segments of the population were thus banished to the outskirts, a trend that shows no sign of ending soon. Sarcelles and Les Chamards date from the same period.

Before decentralization, local authorities were subject to oversight by bureaucrats at the national level. Does this mean that local officials bear none of the blame for what happened? Not entirely. Hubert Dubedout, the mayor of Grenoble whose example inspired a whole generation of young politicians in the late 1970s, notes that many mayors measured their power in terms of cubic feet of asphalt laid down in their cities or in terms of the height of high-rises and number of square feet of public housing built in their suburbs. Dreux is just one of many small cities throughout France paying for the crimes of French city planning.

Nor does Dreux stand out for the large size of its foreign population (roughly 28 percent). Many French cities—and not only the metropolises—have as large or larger a percentage of foreigners living in their midst. Oyonnax (Ain) has a population of 22,800, of whom 7,600, or 30 percent, are of foreign nationality. Saint-Florentin (Yonne) has 6,700 residents, 34 percent of whom are foreigners. Terrasson (Dordogne) has fewer than 6,000 inhabitants but a large Turkish community. Lodève (Hérault) has 10,000 residents, few of whom have foreign nationality; but it does have a community of nearly 2,000 North Africans, *harkis* who are officially French citizens of Lodève but who continue to be regarded as foreigners. The population of Mantes-la-Jolie is 40 percent foreign. It would be possible to cite a long list of large towns, medium-sized cities, bedroom communities serving large urban centers, and sections of Paris with much larger foreign populations than Dreux: the population of the Goutte d'Or section, for instance, is 57 percent foreign, while the thirteenth arrondissement has become Paris' Chinatown.

Similarly, the effects of the recession on Dreux have to be seen in a national context. From the early 1950s to the OPEC oil embargo of 1973, urban growth went hand in hand with prosperity. Overall growth masked growing inequalities. The social changes brought about by mass production, which drains workers from the countryside into the city, from the land to the assembly line, were compensated by a corresponding increase of mass consumption and hopes of social advancement, if not for oneself then at least for one's children. When the recession hit, it was naturally "the city and its outgrowths that initially became the primary theater of economic crisis."[3] Dreux was widely regarded as one of the places in its region hit hardest by the downturn in the economy. Yet its unemployment rate never much exceeded the national average, and the recession in the local economy was by no means as severe as the depression experienced by the cities of the Nord, the Vosges, and Lorraine, which bore the brunt of large-scale industrial collapse.

Dreux Leads, France Follows

By now the reader may be prepared to grant that Dreux was not at all the special case that the media made it out to be at the time of its first notoriety. Yet it is still possible to object that it was in fact in Dreux, and nowhere else, that the National Front scored its breakthrough success in 1983. And it was Dreux that sent Marie-France Stirbois to the National Assembly in 1989. Surely the explanation of these extremist tendencies lies in the local political microclimate. As hypotheses go, that one is attractive and has received a great deal of attention. It has been alleged, for example, that the left-wing administration that ran the city from 1977 to 1983 was responsible for the National Front's victory in September 1983. Writing in *Le Monde* soon after that election, Michel Kajmann blamed the "Gaspard effect" for the 16.7 percent of the vote that went to the Stirbois slate. When I met in a televised debate with Lionel Stoléru, he elaborated on this theme.[4] Dreux, he implied, had invented the National Front out of whole cloth. Without Dreux the Front would not exist. Stoléru, a vehement spokesman for the right-wing opposition, went further: the mayor of Dreux at the time—namely, me—was nothing less than the "creator" of the National Front.

Six years later, when Marie-France Stirbois was elected deputy in the second district of Eure-et-Loir, the outcome was still being blamed on the shortcomings of local politicians both on the right, which had run the city since 1983 and whose candidate (a member of the RPR) had been crushed by Stirbois, and on the left, since the Socialist Party had not even managed to make it to the second round of the 1989 legislative elections. It is worth noting in passing that the same Lionel Stoléru, who later became a minister in the Rocard government, at the time threw his support to the MRG candidate, whose presence in the race was precisely what kept the Socialist candidate out of the second round.

This localist and narrowly political explanation immediately raises a number of questions. Is any city isolated from its nation? Were the outcomes of elections in Dreux determined solely by local causes? Then why did large numbers of people vote for the extreme right in other parts of France? Was the National Front spreading like an epidemic? The answer to all of these questions is a resounding no.

The evidence is clear: where Dreux led, France followed. By-elections held elsewhere after the fall 1983 elections in Dreux confirmed the newfound strength of the National Front. In national elections between 1984 and 1988, the performance of the extreme right in Dreux was not considered newsworthy, because by then the National Front had done better in such places as Mulhouse, Arles, Béziers, Aulnay-sous-Bois, Antibes, Aix-en-Provence, Perpignan, Avignon, Roubaix, Tourcoing, Toulon, and Vénissieux, to say nothing of Marseilles.

Dreux might well have passed up the privilege of revealing what proved to be a major shift in French voting patterns, particularly insofar as the early revelation of that shift in Dreux may have exaggerated its effects nationwide. Circumstances do appear to have affected the results of the voting in Dreux in ways that warrant further discussion.

Local factors tending to increase the extremist vote certainly affected the strategy of the National Front, embodied in Dreux in the person of its secretary-general, Jean-Pierre Stirbois. When he first ran at the head of a slate of candidates in the municipal elections, he was no newcomer to politics. Having run four times in local and national elections over the previous five years, Stirbois was also an incumbent city councillor. The RPR had given him legitimacy some months earlier by including him on the right-wing slate. The September 1983 second-round alliance between the right and the National Front transformed the latter into an accepted part of the local political scene. In Dreux, the National Front thus achieved respectability earlier than elsewhere, on a modest but still significant scale.

Dreux is not cut off from the rest of the world. People in the city listen to the radio, watch television, and read newspapers like people anywhere else. They pay their taxes, ride the trains, attend PTA meetings, work for the government or private business or are self-employed or unemployed, and some own property while others rent. In other words, they live and work much as people do all over France. They also participate in the great national debates, discussing and commenting on the issues at the office, in the factory, or at the local café—and naturally there is disagreement among them.

Let us take another look at the sequence of events. As France returned to work after its summer vacation in the fall of 1983, the mood was somber. The municipal elections of the previous spring had been the first opportunity for voters nationwide to express themselves since the left's victory in the 1981 presidential and legislative elections. As often happens in such midterm elections where no national office is at stake, the voters availed themselves of the opportunity to issue a warning to the government in power, at the time led by Prime Minister Pierre Mauroy. President Mitterrand's period of grace was a distant memory. The tactics and rhetoric of the new majority had at first surprised and soon irritated many, even among its own electorate. Frenetic reforms had failed to improve the daily lives of citizens, especially since early hopes of a major redistribution of wealth had given way, after a year of Socialist rule, to austerity under Jacques Delors's stabilization program.

In by-elections and cantonal elections in early 1982, the left had already begun to lose ground. The March municipal elections resulted in what Henry Tincq characterized as a "trial change of government."[5] Officials at the highest levels took this warning to heart. Would yet another change in economic policy be necessary? After several days of indecision, the government finally chose to move toward an even more rigorous program of austerity. In September 1983, as voters returned from vacation after being forced by new currency controls to cancel foreign travel plans, they found waiting in their stacks of unopened mail not only new tax returns but also pay stubs reminding them that their wages and salaries had been frozen for the past year. It was in these circumstances that Dreux voters went to the polls on 4 and 11 September.

Six years later, when voters in the Eure-et-Loir's second district went to the polls to choose a deputy, all France was in an uproar over the so-called Affair of the Veils. A high-school principal in Creil had refused to allow three girls wearing the traditional Islamic veil to attend school on the grounds that religious symbols are not permitted in French public schools. The minister of education, Lionel Jospin, ruled that the children should be allowed to attend classes and that the principal should hold discussions with the families involved to work out new guidelines. Some intellectuals, issuing their pronouncements from the heights of the Montagne Sainte-Geneviève in the Latin Quarter, compared Jospin's policy to the appeasement of Hitler in 1938, not hesitating to brand the decision an "educational Munich." They were outraged not so much by the substance of the decision as by the clumsy manner in which it was expressed, a manner that reflected a certain embarrassment on the minister's part. For some weeks traditional political differences were set aside as both right and left divided over the issue. To what authorities was a confused voter to turn? Elisabeth Badinter (best-selling author and wife of the Socialist justice minister) and Jean-Marie Le Pen both argued in favor of prohibiting veils in school—obviously for very different reasons. Danielle Mitterrand (the president's wife) and Alain de Benoist (a well-known right-wing journalist) both contended that the wearing of the veil did not violate any law. The groups SOS–Racisme and France–Plus hurled polemics and insults back and forth. The Socialist Party, involved in pre-convention political maneuvering that tolerated all sorts of backstabbing in the chase for delegates, divided into warring pro- and anti-Jospin factions. The din was all but incomprehensible to voters trying to make up their minds about how to vote. All this was unfolding, moreover, against the backdrop of a strike by tax-collection officials, discontent in the ranks of the civil service, and growing dissatisfaction among workers.

Meanwhile the Berlin wall fell, and every night the television news was full of admiration for the courage of the people of the east, rising up to throw off the shackles of totalitarian dictatorship. Paradoxical though it may seem, the Dreux vote and events in East Germany were not unrelated: the media's glorification of German liberation licensed evasions of every kind. Why not indicate, back in Dreux, that taboos had been removed there as well? Voters with no other way to express their uneasiness, or perhaps their wrath, toyed with the idea of casting a "forbidden" ballot. The fact that it was a secret ballot only made it easier to violate the old taboos. Merely by slipping a forbidden ballot for the National Front into the ballot box, one could punish the other candidates, "teach them a lesson." More than one Socialist sympathizer told me, "Sure, I voted for the National Front. Why? Because I've had it up to here with your screw-ups, and one way or another you had to hear about it." I'm prepared to wager that RPR leaders heard the same words from voters on their side of the fence.

The social, political, and media context in which the legislative by-elections of November-December 1989 took place no doubt contributed to the magnitude of the National Front's success in Dreux, Marseilles, and the other places in France where voting took place. Still the fact remains that the party has been making steady progress in election after election in almost all parts of the country. Between December 1989 and March 1990 the National Front gained 7 points in cantonal elections in Tourcoing, 9 in

Mulhouse and Clichy-sous-Bois, 10 in Villeneuve-le-Roi, 12 in Marseilles, 16 in Le Puy, and 19 in Bordeaux. Its rise continued even after the desecration of Jewish graves at Carpentras.[6]

In June 1990 a drama was played out in Villeurbanne very similar to Dreux's in December 1989. The only difference was that in Villeurbanne the left took the place of the right: in the second round of a cantonal by-election, two candidates remained in the running, one from the National Front, the other a Socialist. The RPR candidate had been eliminated. In the Dreux situation, Socialists (who had been in the position in which the RPR found itself in Villeurbanne) had been faced with an agonizing choice. The party's national leaders all offered advice on how to vote. Some argued that everything possible should be done to prevent a victory of the extreme right: so those on the left should vote for the RPR candidate. Others said that it was impossible to cast such a vote and that the best course of action was to abstain. In Villeurbanne, where one seat was at stake, the Socialist Party, now united, called for support from all "republicans." It was the right's turn to vacillate—and admittedly the right was not in good shape. Alain Carignon, who had come to Dreux in 1983 to support the mayoral candidate allied with the National Front, called for a "Republican front" against the extreme right and urged his supporters to vote for the Socialist. Michel Noir, the RPR mayor of Lyons, chose a devious path: by calling for abstention, he effectively strengthened the hand of the National Front.

The Socialist candidate won in Villeurbanne. For the left, Villeurbanne became the "anti-Dreux."[7] Did certain Socialist strategists think they had found the magic potion of their dreams? As long as the right-wing candidate was eliminated in the first round, second-round duels between an extremist and a socialist would assure the left a large majority in the National Assembly. And why shouldn't the same scenario play itself out in other elections? In the presidential election, only two candidates could go on to the second round. Le Pen would then be the ideal opponent, because he would mobilize an opposition including not just the authentic left but a broad democratic front, hopefully a majority. In the euphoria of victory in Villeurbanne, people tended to forget that the National Front candidate there, a university professor who supported the view of Robert Faurisson that the Holocaust never happened, received 37 percent of the vote—hardly an insignificant total.

Blunders or Pathology?

Since 1983, then, the National Front has been climbing steadily. Who is to blame? The question is a recurrent and painful one. Attempts to answer it have generated a spate of editorials, magazine articles, polemics, and dinner-table discussions. At a loss for an explanation, honest democrats have pointed the finger of blame at one another: it is always somebody else's fault.

Some blame Dreux for setting a bad example. Others blame the right for entering into compromise after compromise with the men and ideology of the extreme. Still others blame the left: the extreme right had no power at the polls prior to the Socialist victories in 1981. And then there are the political parties of both sides, which from the top to the bottom of the hierarchy are accused of being cut off from "reality" (it used to be "the masses"). There are those who blame proportional representation for allowing a tiny party to elect deputies to the National Assembly in 1986. Some blame the intellectuals for deserting the public arena. Some blame the media, especially television, for providing Le Pen with a forum and then for not being able to stop him. Some blame antiracists like Harlem Désir, who until recently was the darling of the media but who today is the target of charges along with President Mitterrand, who made generous government financing available to Désir's organization, SOS–Racisme.

Other targets of indiscriminate accusations include those who abandoned volunteer social-service organizations to become professionals serving the welfare state; the weak and faltering trade unions; the decline of civic feeling and ignorance of history; the rise of selfish individualism; the expansion of corporatism.

In the end, the rise of the National Front is blamed on everyone, which amounts to blaming it on no one. Even the most ardent anticommunists have come to the point of longing for the good old days when the Communist Party knew how to keep the masses in line. Yesterday's anticlericals now lament the crisis of the church and worry about the rise of Islam. Ultimately, the situation is said to be a product of the way things are, in the inescapable evolution of industrial society.

The very fact that so many people are asking where the blame lies is proof that the success of the National Front has touched a nerve in France. The party's success is perceived as an anomaly, and that perception implies the existence of some moral norm: "We are accustomed to looking upon anything immoral as abnormal," according to Emile Durkheim. Why does the vote for the party of Jean-Marie Le Pen trigger this kind of reflex? Durkheim suggested in the nineteenth century, that widespread moral outrage is a response to a general social malady: "If, as we have shown, suicide troubles the moral conscience, one cannot help seeing it as a phenomenon of collective pathology."[8]

Like suicide, the extremist vote is shocking because it is a sign of pathology. The National Front has played upon feelings of xenophobia, racism, and antisemitism. Its leader has dismissed the Holocaust and questioned the existence of the gas chambers. All this has focused attention on fairly recent history, on a troubled period about which French men and women steeped in republican culture hoped they could say, "Never again." When the National Front emerged, moreover, few observers believed that the party had a future. It was impossible to imagine that ideas that had led to Auschwitz could find an audience other than among the stubborn vestiges of a "benighted right" on its way to extinction, or at any rate reduced to a fringe-group ideology. At first Le Pen was simply brushed off because it seemed that a party led by such a man could never attract voters beyond the lunatic fringe nostalgic for the days of Hitler and the OAS. This was a man who argued that the use of torture by French forces in Algeria was justified and who told Pierre Mendès France that "as you surely must be aware, you [as a Jew] crystallize in your person a number of patriotic and almost physical repulsions." It seemed impossible—and yet it happened.

Like suicide, the extremist vote flourishes in times of urban crisis and growing individualism and in the vacuum left by the disappearance of old networks of social interaction and solidarity. And like suicide, the National Front is morbid because it poses a threat to democracy. Of course it denies this, just as it denies that it is racist or antisemitic. But it is not even a short step from exclusion based on ethnicity to the suppression of opposing views: these are opposite sides of the same coin.

"All the evidence . . . compels us to view the enormous increase in the number of voluntary deaths over the past century as a pathological phenomenon that grows more menacing every day. What can be done to stop it?"[9] Durkheim's question about suicide in society can also be applied to the National Front. The widespread acceptance of its ideas appears to be the symptom of a malady in the body social, which may prove fatal to democracy. But as Durkheim puts it, "either the word 'malady' is meaningless or it signifies something that can be avoided."

France is not the only nation confronting the problems of urban life, with whole populations marginalized and relegated to ghettos, to what has been called the Fourth World. All of the industrial nations must take drastic steps to rescue their decaying cities. Nevertheless, when the Interministerial Committee on Urban Problems conducted a survey of ten major European cities in need of large-scale urban renewal, a unique feature of the French situation did emerge: in France bureaucrats and politicians tend to be distrustful of the people. In the Netherlands and Great Britain, for example, funds disbursed by the government are made available directly to residents' organizations, whereas "in France the action involves central and local officials while residents are excluded."[10]

This major difference points up the difficulty the French have with carrying out a thorough program of decentralization, which is to say, democratization.

There is a further difficulty in France: urban renewal is a reward meted out to cities that vote correctly. In other words, the authorities act to rehabilitate decaying neighborhoods not because they believe that people have a right to a decent life but because the residents have voted for the party in power. One hopes that central and regional authorities will recognize that it is their duty, apart from any political benefits they may reap, to prevent the development of pockets of poverty and social exclusion. When, moreover, they allow such pockets to develop, it is their duty to repair the damage, which is both of a human and a material order. It has yet to be shown, however, that successful urban renewal in a troubled city is an effective counter to the rise of the National Front. Although both the extremist vote and the number of voters abstaining have attained record levels in decaying urban neighborhoods, neither phenomenon is limited to society's periphery. Extremism and disaffection from politics have permeated the entire society, not only in Dreux but elsewhere. People vote for the National Front or stay home from the polls in wealthy urban neighborhoods, in posh suburbs where all the elevators work, and in that in-between zone of small green lawns where the numerical majority, the "middle class," resides.

No one denies what Prime Minister Rocard told the National Assembly in 1988: mailboxes and elevators must be repaired if daily lives are to be improved. It is not enough, though, just to say that things need fixing; you have to fix them, and do it right. The mailboxes and elevators will soon be useless again if nothing is done about the physical and moral well-being of the people who use them. The riot that took place in October 1990 in a Lyons suburb that had been held up as a model of successful urban renewal is a good example of what I mean.

The consensus on mailboxes and elevators is not only foolish but symptomatic of how empty political debate has become. When the Socialists were elected, their platform was to "change life." Within a few years, that slogan had been forgotten in favor of a government plan whose high point was to make certain that the elevators were working.

The Breakdown of Civic Morality

The principal cause of increased suicide, according to Durkheim, is the loss of a sense of solidarity. If the cause of the extremist vote is similar, then fixing elevators, however laudable as progress, will not stop it. Because voting is a political act, it is up to political society to deal with the malady.

In the Netherlands in the early 1980s, political leaders of both right and left, together with the press and the intellectual community, unanimously agreed to boycott a newly elected extreme-right member of parliament: not one article or picture would be published, not one other member would remain in the chamber when the man spoke. In this way the Dutch established a *cordon sanitaire* around ideas considered to be incompatible with civic morality.

In France, by contrast, it has proved impossible to isolate Le Pen, despite his offensive behavior. The country's politicians have demonstrated no spontaneous will to eliminate him from their midst. But more than that, those who have chosen to combat him, with undeniable sincerity, have only exposed their own uncertainties and differences. Once again Dreux has served as a test case. Prior to the second round of the March 1983 elections, left-wing activists were supported by ordinary citizens from all parts of the political spectrum, people shocked to discover the name of Jean-Pierre Stirbois on the right-wing slate. Some of these people even prepared handwritten flyers setting the word "Democracy" against "Fascism" and "Nazism." Men and women who had never before participated in a political campaign went from door to door to recount, unflinchingly, their experience of the war, the concentration camps, and the Holocaust. Against all expectations, the right was defeated.

The campaign tactics of the left were severely criticized, however, even by some opposed to Le Pen. It was excessive, the critics said, to compare the National Front to fascism. It was foolish and even dangerous to accuse those who voted for Stirbois of being taken in by Nazi ideology. The voters had to be understood, not made to feel guilty. This was an ill-chosen return to the leftist militancy of 1968. The same people who, as student demonstrators in the streets of Paris shouted the slogan "CRS = SS" (equating the French riot police with the Nazi elite guard), now warned that it was "forbidden to forbid" and that everyone should enjoy the right to be different.

In Dreux six years earlier, part of the left, with no candidate in the second round, had been unwilling to vote for the RPR candidate, thereby playing into the hands of the extremists. As soon as one equates the moderate right with the National Front, the last barrier falls: from then on it is no longer possible to exclude the Front on grounds of being undemocratic. It becomes a party just like any other.

The intellectuals also failed to establish a common front against the rise of Le Pen. It was not until the desecration at Carpentras—five years after a panel of academic examiners awarded high honors to former neo-Nazi leader Henri Roques for a thesis denying the existence of the gas chambers—that a group of academics came together to denounce "those who call themselves revisionists and who are nothing but falsifiers of history, or . . . those who publicly support the campaign of xenophobic and racist hatred which, under the banner of nationalism, is nothing but the negation of the authentic values of republican France."[11]

The press also failed to join forces against Le Pen after his first antisemitic attacks on certain journalists. Nor did they boycott the press conference called by the leader of the National Front after Carpentras, even as a huge protest demonstration was being held in Paris. And it is true that even some of the groups founded expressly to combat the ideas of the extreme right sometimes give the impression that they spend more time and energy attacking one another than carrying out their supposed mission: witness the polemics betwen France–Plus and SOS–Racisme.

Civil and Political Society

Intellectuals, the press, and civic associations form the periphery of the political sphere. The men and women elected by the people, from the most obscure to the most illustrious, are at the core. They are the ones who should be questioned about their complacency in the face of rising extremism and their inability to stop it. The questioning should begin with the left, since historically it is the mission of the left to propose an overarching social project. We expect the politicians of the left to tell us how to react to this kind of threat. Why? Because since 1789 the word "left" has implied a vision of the future founded on the struggle against oppression here and now. Who marches beneath the banner of the left today?

In the wake of communism's failure, social democracy alone is capable of expressing the kind of collective project for the future that voters in a democracy are called upon to judge. There is no point in expecting the Socialist Party by itself to come up with a program for ending the economic crisis. France is different from Germany and other European nations: for various historical reasons, the French Socialist Party has not maintained close ties to trade unions, civic organizations, and mutual-assistance groups. It is, or at any rate should be, the very essence of democratic socialism to draw upon all the resources of democratic society.

Even before 1981, Alain Touraine was calling attention to the crisis of the left and warning that it could not be overcome by "an appeal to the parties issuing from a public reduced to a disorganized mass of disappointed voters." He went on to say that to settle for such a vision was "to content oneself with very little for fear of thinking about the situation at all. Henceforth it is not the parties on whom we must rely but the forces at work in the new society. The political parties should be nothing but the representatives of the people. But what constitutes 'the people' today, and who are its enemies? The left often seems afraid to move beyond the vestibules of power. It would do better to look down rather than up and to rediscover the inspiration of every social movement: namely, to join arms with the oppressed, to free the imprisoned, to bring hope to those to whom others preach submission. Social movements need and will continue to need political support and political allies, but priority should be given to the reawakening of social forces."[12] Ultimately, of course, the left did move beyond the vestibules of power into leadership of the state, but it continues to be cut off from, even afraid of, its base. It has remained deaf to the appeals of social movements and to the anguish and hope of its citizens—this at a time when people need to be heard all the more because spatial segregation has deprived large segments of the population of a voice.

To blame political activists and social organizers for deserting their posts and allowing the extreme right to occupy the terrain is to confound cause and effect. The very people who make this charge occupy the terrain just long enough to conduct a survey. Recall the story of the Carré family who moved out of Les Chamards. Should we blame them? What journalist or sociologist would have hung on as long as they did in a slum apartment? "Activist" is not synonymous with "saint." Political people are men and women just like everyone else. Many of them have careers that have not been stymied by the recession, and as their situation improves they can afford to look for better housing. The families left behind are those with multiple handicaps, with no hope of escape. François Dubet has described the lives of these outcasts: theirs is a world with its own vocabulary, codes, and rituals, very different from the rest of society, which speaks the language of newspapers and television—and, *a fortiori*, even more different from the world of the intellectual.[13] The only sound this abandoned segment of the population can make is at the ballot box. The commentators have plenty to say about the 40, 50, or 60 percent who vote for the National Front in a certain neighborhood, village, or town but very little about the 40, 50, or 60 percent who abstain from voting altogether. Abstention, by its very frequency, has become a form of political expression. We have no idea, moreover, how many people have not even bothered to register, let alone vote.

The Fondation pour la Vie Associative (FONDA), commissioned an investigation of the connection between community groups and local politics. The inspiration for this work was Anne Tristan's book *Au front*. She wrote that "in the past, in the neighborhoods of north Marseilles, left-wing community organizations offered a variety of recreational activities. Today, however, these clubs are gone, replaced by a network of Lepenist groups."[14] Accordingly, investigators sought to establish a connection between changes in local community groups and the rise of the National Front in three places where the Front did particularly well: Barr, a small cantonal seat in Alsace; the Pins de Vitrolles housing project in Bouches-du-Rhône; and Londeau, a project of mixed low- and high-rise buildings in Noisy-le-Sec, just outside Paris. The research showed that the decline of left-wing community organizations in these places was directly related to social change. One should be careful not to be misled by the National Front's vote totals and its apparent success at community organizing: "The fact that few National Front activists have established themselves in these areas corroborates the notion that a whole segment of the population is simply estranged from politics and content to remain on the sidelines. The processes of economic decline, social alienation, and intensive urbanization, coupled with a tendency of residents to turn inward or to be prevented from looking outward, probably encourage this kind of political attitude, which can take the form of protest sometimes and abstention at other times."[15]

Consensus versus Democracy

The left consists of more than political parties and their activists. It now has a conductor to lead the orchestra. For the past ten years France has been led by a president of the left. For all but two of those ten years the Socialist Party has enjoyed an absolute or relative majority in the National Assembly.[16] When the left first came to power, it was with the idea that it had a historic mission to fulfill: to carry out essential social reforms quickly before being voted out of office. But ten years in power changed all that: the left had to learn how to govern. There is nothing wrong with that or with having discovered, not without pain, the constraints of the national and international marketplace. But politics is also more than economics, even if it is good politics to ensure a healthy economy. Politics is more than providing social services, even if it is essential that the government design its budget and its laws so as to reduce inequalities and restore equity to the relation between capital and labor.

Shaken by a long economic crisis, French voters have become at least as realistic as the left in the realms of economics and social services. They are no doubt less gullible than they were ten years ago because they have learned to check and recheck the figures. Many have found that the promises made by both sides simply do not add up. Much of the public has come to the conclusion that the government, whether of the right or the left, cannot do much about economic and social problems. Given the tendency to equate right and left in this regard, what do people expect from the left when it is in power? In a word, politics: a memory, certain values and kinds of behavior, and for good measure a modicum of hope.

A memory? The government is not the only keeper of memory nor, to be sure, is it the sole authorized distributor. But the fact is that the national memory is expressed through the medium of government. The government is also responsible for establishing and maintaining the symbols of memory: dates and places. This may seem self-evident, but it is not. The blue, white, and red colors of the French flag once represented warring ideologies, and it was a long time before Bastille Day was accepted as a national holiday. When President Valéry Giscard d'Estaing decided that V-E Day (8 May) would no longer be a holiday, he incurred the wrath of veterans, former prisoners of war, and resistance fighters from World War II. Mitterrand's first act as president was to reinstate the holiday. To inaugurate his first term on 21 May, 1981, he went alone to the Pantheon to visit the tombs of three men: Victor Schoelcher, Jean Jaurès, and Jean Moulin. The deep emotions associated with these heroes of the Resistance enabled spectators to overlook the theatricality of the occasion. What remains of this memory ten years later? No one celebrates the abolition of slavery, although such a commemoration was approved by a law passed on 30 June, 1983 and published in the *Journal officiel*. A statue of Alfred Dreyfus by the sculptor TIM was commissioned, and plans were made to install it in the court of the Ecole Militaire on the spot where Dreyfus was publicly stripped of his rank. But the plans were never carried out, owing to the protests of a handful of army officers, and the statue ended up in a corner of the Tuileries garden. Dreyfus is still awaiting his rehabilitation, though in the meantime the "felonious generals" of the Algerian war have had their pensions restored.

In power, in other words, the left has lost its identity even in its everyday behavior. People expected it to "govern differently," that is, differently from the right. "And what if the great socialist hope were to be squandered in negligence, cowardice, and petty intrigue? What would remain?" So spoke a man well versed in the dangers of power, the first secretary of the Socialist Party, François Mitterrand, in 1976. Negligence was one danger the left managed to avoid. It would be too much to argue, as Laurent Joffrin intimated in his brilliant book, that what worked for the left was not socialist and that what was socialist did not work.[17] There was cowardice, to be sure, but there was also an expansion of liberty. "Petty intrigue" was rife in all the palaces of government, however, and socialist bureaucrats soon accustomed themselves to the perquisites of power, including the ubiquitous official car. In Denmark a government minister damaged his political career beyond repair when, to suit his own schedule, he had a ship's departure delayed for a few minutes. The French lack the democratic reflexes of the nations of northern Europe. They tolerate privilege and accept affronts to equality—or so it is widely believed. Yet did it escape the notice of any Parisian that the celebration of the bicentennial of the French Revolution was marred by traffic jams provoked by all those official vehicles crisscrossing the city with sirens wailing?

Then there has been the stench of financial scandal on the left, which threatens to sully the image of politicians and parties generally and strikes at the very idea of democracy. Shortly after the "strange defeat" of French forces in 1940, the historian Marc Bloch wondered how Vichy could have happened. "Our party machinery gave off a musty odor of tiny cafés and businessmen's dark backrooms."[18] The left has found it difficult to deal with scandalous revelations about the party's financing. Rather than speak openly about the costs of democracy and how to pay for them, court cases were readily dismissed, and the National Assembly voted to give amnesty to those caught raising money by illegal means. In so doing it handed the demagogues a valuable gift. The antiparliamentary theme has been a staple of political demagoguery in France from the time of Boulanger a century ago to Le Pen today. Nowadays, when the parliament itself is of relatively little importance in the political system and the political game is played mainly on television, antiparliamentarism has become antipartyism (as when Le Pen denounced the Gang of Four). The antiparty case is only strengthened by the fact that political leaders appear to be both powerless to solve the pressing problems of the day and cut off from the rest of society, a class apart. Democracy is exigent, however: it insists on being served by individuals who, if not entirely virtuous, are at least subject to the same laws as other people, and it likes its servants to believe in the possibility of a better tomorrow.

Whatever objective or symbolic disappointments the French may have felt about President Mitterrand's first term; however disturbed they may have been by Prime Minister Fabius' remark that Le Pen was asking "good questions"; however bitter a taste may have been left by such scandals as the sabotage of the Greenpeace vessel *Rainbow Warrior* by French agents or the embezzlement of funds by political operatives in the so-called Carrefour du Développement affair—whatever their reservations, the French voted overwhelmingly on 8 May 1988 to reelect Mitterrand to a second seven-year term. They had just endured two years of cohabitation between a Socialist president and an RPR prime minister, and right-wing ideology had made a forceful comeback. The presidential campaign became the occasion for a powerful clash of values, right against left. The president himself set the tone on 22 March when, after much delay, he appeared on television to announce that he would be a candidate for reelection: "I want France to be united, and it will not be if it is taken over by intolerant individuals, by parties that want everything, by clans and gangs . . . I clearly am referring to parties, groups, and factions whose intolerance is apparent every night in the words they choose."

The firmness of the president's words and manner shook politicians for whom consensus had become an obsession. While some on the left remained in doubt that the announcement heralded the beginning of a traditional left-versus-right campaign, the next morning's editorials in the right-wing press made it clear that the speech had hit its mark and the right was closing ranks. When Mitterrand, speaking with conviction, denounced the post-1986 right-wing government's attacks on the freedom and dignity of immigrants, when he reminded his Socialist supporters that he personally favored granting foreigners the right to vote, he was seen as the upholder of democracy and honor. A surge of support for the president followed the successful resolution of the crisis in New Caledonia, where native Kanaks had rebeled against French rule.

Two years later, what had become of the values that had moved so many people to cast their votes for Mitterrand? In November and December 1989, the Socialist candidate in Dreux played down his party affiliation in the hope of drawing votes from a broad spectrum. Meanwhile the RPR candidate borrowed the rhetoric of the National Front. For most voters—those having little or no contact with political activists—it was difficult to interpret the election in terms of left versus right. Only the National Front had a clear identity and a seemingly consistent program. The spectacle that the parties made of themselves in the Eure-et-Loir was a parody of what was going on in Paris. The new government, led by Michel Rocard as prime minister, had sown confusion on the left by adopting a policy of openness toward the right. This, together with the government's silence on social issues, confused the picture. Nor did it help matters that the Socialists could not agree on a direction for the country, while the opposition was hampered by personal rivalries and the lack of a program.

There is every reason to feel anger at the readiness of the traditional right to wink at, or even form alliances with, Jean-Marie Le Pen and his friends. There is every reason to feel outrage at the statement by Charles Pasqua, an RPR leader, that he shared the values of the National Front. There is every reason to feel concern about the friendly letters that former president Giscard addressed to the Front's leader, and concern about Giscard's vote in the European parliament against dissolving the legislative immunity of the man responsible for that obnoxious pun on the name of Durafour. The extreme right is the extreme right. It has been much as it is now for some time, perhaps since the Liberation. General de Gaulle, to whom it is now fashionable to pay homage, did the conservatives a favor by making people forget that, for the right, Vichy and collaboration were a kind of revenge against the Popular Front, not to mention the revolution of 1789.

Furthermore, when the right is in opposition, it has a tendency to become more radical, particularly since it has never fully accepted the concept of alternation in politics. In the spring of 1990 the National Front held its convention in Nice on the same weekend that the right opposition held its conference on immigration at Villepinte, just outside Paris. It would be difficult to say at which of the two the rhetoric was more xenophobic. It is certainly a laudable goal to hope that those on the right who do not share the values of the National Front may one day take a stand against extremism. As a tactic, though, this doesn't take us very far. Michel Noir—who has invoked his own idea of morality through abstention—still belongs to the same party as Charles Pasqua. Bernard Stasi, an appealing centrist whose positions on immigration are diametrically opposed to those of Le Pen, continues to place himself on the right, alongside avowed Lepenists, despite the hard time he was given at Villepinte by his supposed allies.

That the so-called moderate right has been willing to tolerate the extreme right is a worrisome clue to the state of the nation. It indicates that the "authentic values of republican France"—values in the name of which the group of academics called for isolation of those who would deny the Holocaust—are not shared by all the parties who invoke republicanism and democracy in their very names. Even more worrisome, in my view, is the fact that the whole French political system, including the left, has shifted to the right, adopting a vocabulary and issues given currency by what ten years ago was little more than a sectarian fringe group, a group held at bay precisely because it embodied a denial of the republican ideal. President Mitterrand has spoken of a "threshold of tolerance." The prime minister has told hungry people that France "cannot accommodate all the world's misery," and the government continues to support dictatorial regimes in Africa. Before a conference on racism could be held, moreover, the Socialist Party issued a communiqué that reads like a renunciation of the proposal to extend local voting rights to foreign residents. This is tantamount to deserting the battlefield under fire—a humiliating and dishonorable retreat, which further confused Socialist activists and sympathizers.

Writing in *Le Monde,* Philippe Boucher was on target: "Poor Socialists! The party had already lost its influence on the government's policy, and now it is no longer even allowed to dream . . . It has been an open secret for ages that the government's economic policy was inspired by the right, and now the extreme right is dictating its conditions in regard to foreigners. While it is true that it was the right that insisted on a commitment (from the government, not the Socialist Party) against granting foreigners the right to vote, it did so under pressure from the extreme right, for which, on this issue, it acts as the frightened spokesman. The domino strategy continues to rule French politics, and M. Le Pen has more concrete influence on the government than does the principal party in the governing coalition."[19]

In the 1880s France chose a republican form of government in preference to monarchy and conservatism. Led by Léon Gambetta, the son of Italian immigrants, republicans skillfully exploited divisions in the monarchist camp and subtly used the machinery of parliament to defeat the counterrevolutionary camp. But at no point did they renounce their fundamental convictions. Indeed, it was because they affirmed those convictions in both caucuses and classrooms that the Republic triumphed. To be sure, it was a republic open to anyone prepared to pledge his or her allegiance. But it was by no means a united France, not in political terms: democracy is predicated on choice, on open debate. "It is good, it is healthy," wrote Marc Bloch after going underground during World War II, "that opposing social philosophies engage in free combat in a free country. Given the state of society today, it is inevitable that different classes should have different interests and that they should be aware of their antagonism. The nation's woes begin when the legitimacy of such conflict is no longer understood."[20]

Counterrevolution is no longer on the horizon in France. Social antagonisms are no longer perceived, in corporate society, as the locomotive of history. The left no longer defines itself as the representative of one class opposed to another, but simply as the adversary of the right. And the moderate right will on occasion enter into alliance with the extreme right because its only objective is, conversely, to beat the left. French voters, across the spectrum from right to left, have been reduced to giving their votes to representatives whose positions are unclear and, increasingly, tainted by verbal concessions to the extreme right. More and more of those voters look upon elections as a kind of ritual that does not concern them. Right and left cannot be political adversaries unless there are clear values behind the partisan rhetoric and a clear program that voters can either accept or reject. Le Pen has prospered because he, at least, shows the voters an adversary they can readily identify: the other, the immigrant, the foreigner within.

Elsewhere in Europe the extreme right was slower to mobilize. What accounts for this difference? Not all of the countries in question are republics, and none claims to be the birthplace of human rights. What they do share, however, is a democratic culture based on respect for all citizens, each of whom is expected to take part in the nation's government.

Take the Netherlands. An amendment to the provisions of the constitution governing political rights is currently being drafted. This is the second such amendment. The first, adopted in 1983, granted foreigners the right to vote in local elections and to run for local office. The new amendment will extend this right to national elections. In France, debate on this issue stirs powerful passions. In the Netherlands, it has focused mainly on ways to increase the political participation of all residents, always a difficult task. The Dutch political system reacted to extremism not by attempting to prevent a xenophobic party from expressing its views but by erecting a "civic dike" around its ideas. That citizenship should be based on residence rather than nationality seems logical in a country whose population stems from the soil of both Europe and the former Dutch colonies.[21]

The belief that living and working in a place and paying taxes there should give a person the right to participate in political decisions is a natural corollary of this idea. But it is not enough to make democracy work. The nation's institutions must also have confidence in every citizen. They must make all citizens feel that they have a right not only to choose representatives but actually to shape their own destiny as participants in and not merely subjects of government. In the Netherlands as well as in Great Britain, even under conservative governments, money for urban renewal is given to the residents of the affected neighborhoods. Recognizing the rights of each individual also implies shunning whoever questions those rights. The debate between left and right continues unabated—but democratic values are so natural a part of the debate that even the most conservative elements of the right can join with the left in a determination to uphold them.

Just as the rise of the extreme right is not simply a protest against "politics as usual," so too mere tactics cannot stop it. Le Pen has been able to disguise his true ideology behind hostility to immigration because both the right and the left—in other words, the collective voice speaking in the name of the French people—have proved unable to reveal to the nation that the extremist enterprise is harmful to its health. What politics and politicians must do is to establish democracy. Politics must be put back in the hands of citizens, and equal rights in matters of common interest must be secured for every neighborhood of every town as well as for France as a whole. To create such unity is an enormous challenge, but it must be met if everyone from the conductor leading the orchestra to the person sitting in the last row of the concert hall is to be equally moved by the music they hear. Solidarity is a product of the conviction that every citizen, whether of a village or a nation, shares the same rights and duties in confronting the common destiny. Gambetta and the republicans of the Third Republic rallied France around the democratic ideal, but the adherence to republican values is still not perfect: more than a century after the inception of the Third Republic, democracy has yet to capture the minds and mores of the French. Those who claim to belong to the forces of progress must respond to this challenge.

If they are to be successful, they would do well to cultivate memory without succumbing to nostalgia. The France of the late twentieth century is at once the France of Durkheim and the

France of Raï (Algerian pop music). The old and the new are mingled. Society is in some ways still a pyramid, but there are signs that it is beginning to resemble a mosaic as well. The working class has disintegrated, but the reality of exploitation lives on. The nation-state remains, but it has been weakened by the broader circulation of workers, capital, and information. The demand for democracy in cities is henceforth inseparable from the demand for democracy in a realm that transcends national boundaries.

Today's citizens remember not only Jules Ferry's words about equality of opportunity but also those of François Mitterrand, spoken at Cancun, about the dignity and rights of people of all nationalities. We believe in justice and in human rights: France, after all, has been considered the birthplace of these universal principles.

Even if Dreux irresistibly calls to mind the small German city that gave two-thirds of its vote to the Nazis in 1933, even if today's ideological tendencies are in disturbing ways similar to tendencies perceptible in the Weimar Republic, the triumph of extremism is not inevitable. But if it is to be avoided, what is happening in Dreux, in the heart of France, must be heard as an appeal, as a cry for help.

Notes

Revisiting Dreux

1. *L'Echo républicain,* 4 March 1990.
2. At the December 1989 European summit meetings in Strasbourg, Chancellor Helmut Kohl of Germany and President François Mitterrand of France reportedly discussed the National Front's electoral victory in Dreux the Sunday before. "What would the French say," Kohl is said to have asked, "if an extremist right-wing party scored a similar victory in West Germany?"
3. According to Jérôme Jaffré, vice-president of the polling organization SOFRES, quoted in *Libération,* 8 November 1983. Several months before the European parliamentary elections of June 1984, in which Jean-Marie Le Pen's National Front obtained 11 percent of the vote, political scientists were still underestimating the party's influence. For instance, René Rémond compared the National Front to the extremist, short-lived Poujadists of the 1950s. Reminding his readers that the conservative Union and Fraternity slates had garnered only 12.5 percent of the vote, he remarked: "We still have a long way to go before we reach that point." See *Le Point,* 13 February 1984.
4. Throughout much of the period described here, French legislative and presidential elections took place in two stages. In the *premier tour,* or first round, many parties run slates of candidates. Only those receiving a certain minimum percentage of the votes cast are eligible to continue to the second round, which takes place two weeks later. In the interim, the parties often engage in negotiations over which candidates will continue. If there are, say, two left-wing candidates in a district, the less well-placed candidate

will normally drop out of the second round and urge voters to switch to the other leftist. This informal system, often referred to as "republican discipline," has historically worked to ensure that a multiparty system functions in many ways like a two-party system. One of the problems that arose in Dreux, however, was that the parties of the so-called traditional or democratic or legitimate right were tempted to enter into an alliance with the extremist National Front in order to defeat the left, thus raising the possibility that the pursuit of partisan advantage might offer a foothold to a party perceived by many people as fundamentally antidemocratic.

5. On the day Marie-France Stirbois was elected deputy in the Eure-et-Loir, another National Front candidate defeated a dissident socialist in the previously socialist canton of Salon-de-Provence. Two other cantonal elections, in Finistère and the Nord, confirmed the progress made by the party of the extreme right.

6. Goguel and Jaffre both quoted in *Le Figaro*, 28 November 1989.

7. For example, an article by Olivier Roy in the February 1990 issue of *Esprit* is mistaken even about such easily checked matters as election results.

8. *L'Evénement du jeudi*, 30 November–6 December 1989.

9. W. S. Allen, *The Nazi Seizure of Power: The Experience of a Single German Town, 1930–1935* (New York: Franklin Watts, 1965); published in France as *Une Petite Ville nazie* (Laffont, 1967). Thalburg was the name chosen by Allen to disguise the city of Northeim in Lower Saxony. When the book came out in German translation, the magazine *Der Spiegel* revealed the town's true identity.

1. Intruders in the City

1. Quoted in Charles Maillier, *Dreux et le pays Drouais* (Dreux, published by the author, 1958).

2. Jacques Rossiaud, "Crise et consolidation, 1330–1530," in Georges Duby, ed., *Histoire de la France urbaine*, vol. 2: *La Ville médiévale*, p. 583.

3. Quoted in Maillier, *Dreux*, p. 202.

4. Fernand Braudel, *L'Identité de la France*, vol. 1 (Paris: Arthaud-Flammarion, 1986), pp. 65–66; available in English (HarperCollins, 1989).

5. Antoine Prost, "Les Monuments aux morts," in Pierre Nora, ed., *Les Lieux de mémoire*, vol. 1: *La République* (Paris: Gallimard, 1984).

6. Maillier, *Dreux*, p. 69.

7. Daniel Cordier, in vol. 1 of *Jean Moulin, l'inconnu du Panthéon*, thoroughly examines Moulin's role as prefect of the Eure-et-Loir from February 1939 to November 1940.

8. Jean Moulin, *Premier combat* (Paris: Minuit, 1947), pp. 28–29.
9. Maurice Viollette, *Notes* (Chartres: Lainé et Tanté, 1950), p. 160.
10. First elected deputy from Dreux in 1902, Viollette held a seat in parliament continuously through 1956, except for the periods 1919–1924 and 1938–1945. He served as mayor of Dreux from 1908 to 1959, as *conseiller général* (regional representative) from 1904 to 1960, and as president of the Conseil Général from 1921 to 1960. He was removed from his various local offices by the Vichy government.
11. Viollette, *Notes,* p. 166.
12. *L'Echo républicain,* 14 August 1989.
13. Network FR3, *Rencontres,* January 1990.
14. Today Nomel is little more than a memory in Dreux. Nearly all the firm's activities had been transferred to the Orne region by the fall of 1990.
15. Claude Parry, "Un Exemple de décentralisation industrielle, la dispersion des usines de 'la Radiotechnique' à l'ouest de Paris," *Annales de géographie,* 1963, p. 157.
16. For an excellent account of the slow unification of France's disparate regions, see Eugen Weber, *Peasants into Frenchmen* (M. Stanford, 1976).
17. Quoted in Michel Pierre, *Le Dernier Exil: histoire des bagnes et des forçats* (Paris: Gallimard, 1989), pp. 16–17.
18. Quotations and other information taken from Laurent Percerou, "Surveillance et réinsertion des bagnards et détenus libérés à Dreux, 1820–1870," master's thesis, University of Tours, 1984.
19. Michel Michel, "Ville moyenne, ville-moyen," *Annales de géographie,* 1977, p. 660.
20. Parry, "Un Exemple de décentralisation industrielle," p. 155.
21. *Le Monde,* 17 July 1971.

2. Crucible and Crisis

1. Jean-Jacques Carré, Paul Dubois, and Edmond Malivaud, *Abrégé de la croissance française* (Paris: Seuil, 1973), p. 263.
2. Pierre-Adrien Hamelin, "Dreux: croissance urbaine et évolution politique," master's thesis, University of Tours, 1988.
3. *Liaisons centre,* December 1989.
4. *L'Echo républicain,* 13 February 1990.
5. Pierre Bourdieu in *Le Nouvel Observateur,* 14–20 June 1990.
6. On the history of this district and its population, see Daniel Bourdon and Agnès Vachette, "La Cité Prod'homme à Dreux," in *Droit de cité, à la rencontre des habitants délaissés* (Paris: L'Harmattan, 1986).

7. *Le Monde,* 20 February 1990.
8. Pierre Bourdieu, "Un Signe des temps," *Actes de la Recherche en sciences sociales,* March 1990.
9. "Galley slaves" was the analogy that came to François Dubet's mind. His book about problem children is entitled *Galère* (Paris: Fayard, 1987).
10. "Missions locales d'insertion sociales et professionnelles des jeunes" were created in many French cities after Bertrand Schwartz drafted a report on the problem of unemployed youth in 1982. Their role was to provide guidance to young people between the ages of sixteen and twenty-five. The idea was to do real missionary work, not to act like a standard bureaucracy. Unfortunately, despite a few exceptions, most of the local missions forgot Schwartz's philosophy and served primarily as employment agencies for youthful jobseekers.
11. Quoted in *La Vie,* 21 June 1990.
12. Until 1980, prefectoral statistics combined Dreux with the neighboring commune of Vernouillet.
13. Inaugurated in 1977, this policy was strongly criticized by the left. In 1984, however, the government of Socialist Pierre Mauroy revived the return subsidy program, though with little success.
14. Bourdieu, "Un Signe des temps."
15. The 1982 census counted 3.7 million foreigners in France, but in December of the same year the minister of the interior released figures showing that more than 4.4 million residence permits had been issued. One reason for the discrepancy is that foreigners are not required to surrender their residence permits when they return home (unless they receive a subsidy to defray the cost of the journey).
16. Gérard Noiriel, *Le Creuset français* (Paris: Seuil, 1988), pp. 172–173.
17. Selcuck Kadioglu, "Essai d'analyse de l'immigration turque sur le quartier des Chamards à Dreux," typescript, Institut Parmentier, 1984.
18. *Paris-Match,* 14 December 1989.
19. Article 23 of the Code of Nationality states: "A child, whether legitimate or natural, born in France and at least one of whose parents was also born there, is French." Hence a child born in France to Algerian parents is French at birth if either parent was born in a part of Algeria that was considered a département of France prior to the granting of independence in 1962.
20. Abdemmalek Sayad, "Les Enfants illégitimes," *Actes de la Recherce en science sociale,* January, March, and April 1979.
21. Jean-Pierre Stirbois was neither a resident of Dreux nor a registered voter there. He lived in Neuilly-sur-Seine outside Paris.

22. *L'Echo républicain,* August 12, 1983.
23. Pierre Milza, "Le Racisme anti-italien en France, la tuerie d'Aigues-Mortes, 1893," *L'Histoire,* March 1979. Ralph Schor, *L'Opinion française et les étrangers, 1919–1939* (Paris: Publication de la Sorbonne, 1985).
24. Fernand Braudel, *L'Identité de la France,* vol. 1 (Paris: Arthaud-Flammarion, 1986).
25. Colloquium organized by a club of supporters of one-time Socialist prime minister Laurent Fabius on the theme "Espace 89," March 1985. The proceedings have been published under the title *L'Identité française* (Paris: Tierce, 1985).
26. Claude Lévi-Strauss, *L'Identité* (Paris: Grasset, 1976).
27. Jules Michelet, *Tableau de la France,* 1833.
28. On this point see Noiriel, *Le Creuset français,* p. 505.
29. Braudel, *L'Identité de la France,* p. 11.
30. Ernest Renan, "Qu'est-ce qu'une nation?" Lecture delivered at the Sorbonne on 11 March 1882.

3. The Irresistible Rise of the Right

1. *L'Action républicaine* was founded by Viollette in 1902. It was acquired by Robert Hersant in 1959 and still publishes today. See Françoise Gaspard, *Maurice Viollette, editorialiste et homme politique* (Paris: Edijac, 1986).
2. *L'Action républicaine,* 28 May 1958.
3. *Paris-Match,* 14 December 1989.
4. *La République du centre,* 3 March 1978.
5. The oas (for Secret Armed Organization) was a group within the French military that conspired against, and at times violently opposed, the French government's efforts to negotiate an end to the war in Algeria.
6. *Le Parisien libéré,* 5 March 1953.
7. *La République du centre,* 2 October 1982.
8. Michel Michel, *Développement des villes moyennes: Chartres, Dreux, Evreux* (Paris: Publications de la Sorbonne, 1984), p. 248.
9. The udf was an alliance of the Parti Républicain, the cds, and several other smaller centrist parties.
10. *La République du centre,* 23 November 1982.
11. Ibid., 28 December 1982.
12. See Françoise Gaspard and Claude Servan-Schreiber, *La Fin des immigrés* (Paris: Seuil, 1984).
13. Quoted in *L'Action républicaine,* 14 June 1983.
14. *Le Nouvel Observateur,* 4 March 1983.

15. Quoted in Joseph Algazy, *L'Extrême-Droite en France, 1965–1984* (Paris: L'Harmattan, 1989), p. 61.
16. *Parachutage* is the French term for the practice of using "safe" districts to elect nonresident party officials to the National Assembly.
17. Two exit polls were conducted in Dreux on 3 December 1989: *Figaro*-IFOP and BVA-*Libération*. Having talked with the polltakers, I was able to gauge some of the problems they faced: the very low level of voter participation made it difficult to choose a representative sample, particularly since the number of those refusing to answer was high. Suggestive as the polls are, the results are to be interpreted with caution.
18. See Noma Mayer and Pascal Perrineau, *Le Front national à découvert* (Paris: Presses de la Fondation Nationale des Sciences Politiques, 1989).
19. Anne Tristan, *Au front* (Paris: Gallimard, 1987).

Rediscovering the Citizen

1. Guy Burgel, "Urbanisation des hommes et des espaces," *Histoire de la France urbaine,* vol. 5, p. 141.
2. Ibid., p. 175.
3. Marcel Roncayolo, "Conclusion," *Histoire de la France urbaine,* p. 639.
4. *Antenne 2,* 17 March 1984.
5. Henri Tincq, "Raisons et conséquences d'une sanction," *Revue politique et parlementaire,* April 1983.
6. In May 1990 Jewish graves were vandalized in the cemetery at Carpentras (near Aix-en-Provence). Although the violation was probably the work of local youths, the National Front was widely blamed, and much of the commentary on the event alluded to the climate of xenophobia and antisemitism fostered by Le Pen's party.
7. To borrow an expression from Gilbert Chabrous, the mayor of Villeurbanne, in *Libération,* 19 June 1990.
8. Emile Durkheim, *Le Suicide* (Paris: Presses Universitaires de France, 1986), p. 413.
9. Ibid., p. 424.
10. *Libération,* 22 June 1990.
11. Those who signed this appeal, issued by Jacques Le Goff, Michel Broué, François Jacob, Madeleine Rebérioux, Laurent Schwartz, and Pierre Vidal-Naquet, pledged to boycott any academic organization or meeting that admitted people professing revisionist or racist ideas.
12. Alain Touraine, *L'Après-Socialisme* (Paris: Grasset, 1980), p. 273.
13. François Dubet, *Galère* (Paris: Fayard, 1987).

14. Tristan, *Au front,* p. 85.
15. "Pratique associative et vie politique locale," FONDA, Newsletter 72–73, May 1990.
16. These words were written in 1991. In 1993 the right obtained a majority in the National Assembly and Edouard Balladur became prime minister; Mitterrand continued as president.
17. Laurent Joffrin, *La Gauche en voie de disparition* (Paris: Seuil, 1984).
18. Marc Bloch, *L'Etrange Défaite,* new ed. (Paris: Gallimard, 1990), p. 189; available in English trans. (Hippocrene Books, 1967).
19. *Le Monde,* 26 May 1990.
20. Bloch, *L'Etrange Défaite,* p. 194.
21. Similarly, in Great Britain immigrants born in any Commonwealth country can vote in British elections and run for office.

Index